Praise for Mallika Chopra
and *Just Breathe*:

"How fun to read this book with my kids
and all be mindful—and happier—together!"
—Jennifer Garner

"*Just Breathe* is a gift for the whole family. With fun illustrations
and simple steps, this book will empower you to feel more in control, to
genuinely connect with others, and to approach life with peace and joy."
—Dr. Shefali Tsabary, clinical psychologist and author of
the *New York Times* bestseller *The Conscious Parent*

"*Just Breathe* is the book I wish I had growing up."
—Tara Stiles, founder of Strala Yoga

"Chopra opens the door to a direct discovery of how good
it feels to be less anxious, healthier, and experience a more
balanced way of life. Starting meditation young, in adolescence,
is a lifelong set up for health peace and thriving."
—Dr. Lisa Miller, author of *The Spiritual Child* and professor and founder,
Spirituality and Mind-Body Institute, Columbia University, Teachers College

"*Just Breathe* will help you find the inner power to better
connect with friends and family, be healthier and happier, and
succeed at what you want to do."
—Congressman Tim Ryan

"This wonderful book is a real treasure for kids of all ages. . . . It is a totally
beautiful and joyful approach to contemplative practice in real life!"
—Rev. Joan Jiko Halifax, Abbot, Upaya Zen Center

"A charming and engaging book of life skills that speaks
directly to tweens themselves, not through intermediaries like
their parents or teachers. Mallika's wonderful new book is
an essential addition to your child's bookshelf!"
—Susan Kaiser Greenland,
author of *Mindful Games* and *The Mindful Child*

JUST BREATHE

MEDITATION, MINDFULNESS, MOVEMENT, AND MORE

MALLIKA CHOPRA

Foreword by Deepak Chopra, MD
Illustrated by Brenna Vaughan

RP | KIDS
PHILADELPHIA

Running Press Kids
Hachette Book Group
1290 Avenue of the Americas, New York, NY 10104
www.runningpress.com/rpkids
@RP_Kids

Printed in China

First Edition: August 2018

Published by Running Press Kids, an imprint of Perseus Books, LLC,
a subsidiary of Hachette Book Group, Inc. The Running Press Kids name
and logo is a trademark of the Hachette Book Group.

The Hachette Speakers Bureau provides a wide range of authors for speaking events.
To find out more, go to www.hachettespeakersbureau.com or call (866) 376-6591.

The publisher is not responsible for websites (or their content)
that are not owned by the publisher.

Print book cover and interior design by Frances J. Soo Ping Chow.

Library of Congress Control Number: 2017958095

ISBNs: 978-0-7624-9158-2 (paperback), 978-0-7624-9157-5 (ebook)

1010

10 9 8 7 6 5

TO TARA AND LEELA,

My loves. My life.
My teachers.

—MOM

TABLE OF CONTENTS

• • • • •

FOREWORD

Dear Kids:

This book is written by Mallika Chopra, my daughter, who learned to meditate at the age of nine.

As you approach your teenage years, you may experience turbulence in your mind and emotions because your body will be changing rapidly. Teenage years are some of the most important years preparing you for adulthood and the life you want to create. This book will help you get through some of the turbulent times feeling less overwhelmed, more in control, and, generally, happier.

Why should you learn meditation, mindfulness, breathing, and movement? These are simple techniques that go back thousands of years in wisdom traditions all over the world. These skills have allowed people to get in touch with their own inner beings. You are more than your body and your mind. Your body and mind help you take in information and experience it as the physical world. Your innermost being is the part of you that can control your body and can choose how you interpret experiences. By getting in touch with your true self, you will harness the powers of intuition, insight, imagination, creativity, and intention. These are the qualities of your soul.

There is nothing more important for human beings than to know themselves and to have self-love. If you have these two things, you will enjoy a life without much chaos or stress; you will experience the best friendships and relationships; and you will be able to fulfill all your dreams.

The world we live in is full of tremendous opportunity. If you watch the news or hear your parents and teachers talk, you will realize that our world right now also seems confused, violent, chaotic, and self-destructive. You are the hope for the future of this world. If you are joyful, the world will be joyful. If you are at peace, the world will be at peace. If you experience love, the world will be loving. You will be the role model and leader for your families, communities, and nations.

Read the simple steps outlined in this book. Do not stress if what you are doing is right or wrong; just follow the instructions and the exercises and have fun.

Deepak Chopra, M.D.

Mom, Tara & Leela

Dad, me, and my brother

My nephew Krishan meditating

me and my girls

Dad & me

our dog, Yoda

My family

INTRODUCTION

Do you have a place where you feel safe, happy, and quiet?

Perhaps it's a physical space—somewhere in your home, a hidden corner that no one else knows about, or a place outside where you can run, twirl, and laugh without any worries.

Perhaps it's not a physical space, but instead is the time you spend with a friend, a sibling, or a parent? Maybe it's those moments you chat with your sister before you both fall asleep, or when you throw a baseball with a friend and the time flies by.

Or, perhaps it is when you are by yourself, reading, drawing, or daydreaming about nothing in particular—moments when your mind and body feel rested, when you're not thinking about the past or worried about the future.

Maybe you are thinking that you don't have that place in your life . . .

And you are wondering if you even need it.

Research shows that when you find that quiet place, your body and brain are healthier, you feel more in control, and you are happier. And for many people, being able to feel that peace inside of themselves helps them worry less and deal better with tough situations.

The intent of this book is to help you find an anchor, inside yourself, that is safe, happy, and quiet—and to help you tap into it, and find it, whenever you need it.

Who Am I, and Why Am I Writing This Book?

• • • • •

My name is Mallika.

I am a mom of two girls named Tara and Leela. While I am writing this book, Tara is fifteen years old and Leela is twelve. Everything in this book is from our personal experience.

When I was nine years old, my parents taught my younger brother and me how to meditate. I will explain meditation more in the following pages, but basically it was a way that I could quiet my mind, feel less stressed, and feel more in control of my life. There are lots of other practices in this book that have helped me and my girls deal with stress, sleep better, manage friendships, be more in control, and feel confident about expressing what we want.

I feel grateful for the wisdom that my parents passed on to me and that I can pass on those ideas to my kids, their friends, their parents, and others who may be interested. I hope you find them helpful, too. I hope as you read and practice them that you share your experiences with the people closest to you. In fact, you may find that you can help others in ways you didn't know you could before!

What Are We Talking about Here?

• • • • •

There are certain techniques that can help you feel better. The four main techniques are called meditation, mindfulness, yoga, and motivation.

You may have heard these words from your parents, from a teacher at school, or from people in the media, but you may not be exactly sure what they really are. Here are some super quick descriptions for you:

- Meditation helps you quiet your mind.
- Mindfulness helps you become more aware of your body, thoughts, and surrounding environment.
- Yoga moves your body to let go of tension, breathe, relax, be more connected, and get more energy.
- Motivation is using positive thoughts to feel happier and to achieve your goals.

Intents are also an important part of meditation and mindfulness. An intent expresses what you want in your life. It's different from the material things you may want, like new clothes or video games or tickets to an event. Rather, it is the qualities you want to experience every day—like being healthy, happy, and connected to friends and family.

Perhaps you have tried some of these techniques without even knowing it! Maybe your teacher has you breathe in and out before a test. Maybe your sports coach asks you to close your eyes and envision winning a game before you play. Perhaps your mom asks you to notice how you feel after you are mean to your younger sibling or friend. Perhaps you twist and stretch, turn and balance, and then lie down at the end of a dance class to relax your muscles. Maybe you say a prayer during your religious holidays where you ask for health and happiness for your friends and family.

Just because it's easy to do these things doesn't mean they aren't powerful.

Believe it or not, sometimes just taking a deep breath or thinking about what you are grateful for can change your whole day (and improve your whole life)!

What Is Stress?

• • • • •

Stress is when your mind and body don't feel good.

Stress comes in lots of forms:

· Fear

· Worry

· Anxiety

When you are stressed, different things happen to you:

· You may have trouble breathing.

· Your heart beats faster.

· Your hands and body begin to sweat.

· Your body tenses up.

· Your mind gets foggy.

And if you are stressed a lot, your body reacts by getting tired, overwhelmed, and sometimes sick. Perhaps you get headaches or have trouble sleeping. Or, you can get sad and depressed and feel hopeless at times.

If, as a kid, you can learn to manage your stress early on, not only can you get through your days better, but you will set the stage to be healthier and happier when you grow up!

Understanding Your Brain and Your Body

· · · · ·

Let's take a moment and understand how your brain and body react to stress.

Thousands of years ago, humans had to survive with little shelter and to protect themselves against wild animals and extreme weather. When early humans were confronted with dangerous situations, their bodies and brains went into survival mode.

So, say you, as an early human, came across an angry tiger! Your body would immediately get ready to fight or run away! This is called the *fight-or-flight* response.

Your brain, sensing danger, would make your heart beat faster, send more blood to your muscles, and tell you to breathe faster so that you would have the strength and energy to escape or fight! Once you had dealt with the situation, your body and brain would return to normal, and you then would rest to recover.

Or, if you were really scared, perhaps you would just *freeze*, and well then, you would really be in trouble. You would hold your breath and your body would shake with fear.

Fast-forward to today. Most of us are not in the wild, fighting angry tigers. Danger may not seem as dramatic, but your body and brain still react in this same way. When someone is mean to you on the playground, when you don't know how to solve a math problem, or when your parents are fighting, you still may feel vulnerable. And so your brain may react by sending the chemicals to the body to fight off the situation or to just freeze. This creates a sense of stress and tension, and even though inside you may feel that it's dangerous, it is not as real as fighting a wild tiger. But your body doesn't realize that! It reacts the same way as it would in that situation. And often you don't take the time to let your body and brain recover after the "danger" has gone away.

Instead of just letting your brain react automatically to a situation—like that fight-or-flight or freeze reaction—you can help your brain take a pause and react smarter and calmer, and then come up with better solutions to handling difficult situations.

If you know how to deal with stress, then when someone calls you a bad name, or when you feel you have too much homework, or when you are left out of a group situation, you won't automatically get upset or depressed. You know, instead, that you can access that safe, happy place to make a better plan. And you don't let the stress build up! Instead, you give your brain and body time to rest and recover, and to stay strong.

How Meditation Can Help You

. . . . .

Meditation teaches your brain how to stay calm in stressful situations. It helps you find that quiet, safe, and happy place inside yourself and to get to it whenever you need it.

This is how meditation works: Your mind is usually racing with thoughts. One thought makes you think another thought, which makes you think another thought. When you meditate, you slow down racing thoughts. You create more peace inside. You realize that you can control your reactions or choose your next thoughts.

Meditation helps you pause.

So when you are in a panicked situation, as long as you don't have to escape a wild tiger, you can take a moment to think if there is a better solution.

Meditation also gives your brain rest.

When you rest your brain, like when you rest your body when you sleep, your brain works better. When your brain is rested, you can make better decisions.

So meditation can help you feel more in control of immediate stressful situations, but, more importantly it can make you stronger for longer-term challenges.

Building a Habit

· · · · ·

When you do something over and over again, it becomes easier to do. That's why when you try new things, you have to practice to get better and soon things become easier. Like when you are learning to ride a bike, it may take a while to figure out how to balance—and how you can move and balance at the same time. With more practice, you find that you can easily ride a bike.

With the exercises in this book, you need to have practice and have patience. The more you do the exercises, the easier they will become.

Think of a peaceful forest that no one has ever visited. At first there is no clear path for you to walk down. You need to clear the way, and it may be difficult to make it through the bushes, the mud, and other things. But with each walk down the same way, the path becomes clearer and easier to walk on.

Your body and mind are similar to a path in the woods. Your mind can be full of stress and worries. Your body can feel tension that builds up. The first time you try some of these exercises it may even feel a bit weird. But if you find it helpful at all, know that the more you do it, the easier it gets.

How to Do the Exercises in This Book

· · · · ·

One of the most important lessons of this book is to learn how to relax.

While doing the exercises to come, remember: don't get nervous about doing them in any exact way. Your body will always make sure you breathe. Your mind will always have racing thoughts. You can't really be bad at breathing, meditating, or moving!

The point of this book is to give you some exercises and tips on how you can use your breath to calm down and to feel more in control of your thoughts.

Think of this book as a map. It will help guide you to different places, but sometimes you may choose a different path. That is okay.

In fact, it's great!

Part of the goal of this book is to help you find your own voice and your own

path—to know how your body and mind react to situations and to know how you can manage your own situations better.

For the exercises in this book, choose one at a time. Read the exercise first. Then, put the book aside and try it by yourself.

Or . . .

You may want to ask a parent, caretaker, sibling, or friend to read the exercise to you and then do it with them.

Don't worry if you do it a different way. And if you forget how to do it, even in the middle of doing it, you can just look at the book again!

When you want to time yourself, you can use a clock or alarm with a sound that is soothing to you. If the exercise says to do it for five minutes, and you decide you are done after two minutes, that's perfectly fine. Or you may find you want to do it for fifteen minutes. That's okay, too!

You may also find it helpful to write notes or draw how you feel after doing an exercise or jot down what you learned about while doing it. It may be helpful to keep a journal of your reflections and to set intents (what you want) for the future. It can always be fun and enlightening to look back at these, remembering some of your struggles and what practices helped you on your journey. It is empowering to know that you have grown, overcome challenges, and solved problems.

Some exercises may be helpful, and some you may want to skip. That, too, is okay. Do whatever feels most comfortable for you.

THAT SAFE, HAPPY PLACE

Let's do an exercise to think about when you feel happy and safe. Read through the exercise first, and then try it by yourself. It's all right if you don't remember the exact sequence, as you can adjust it to do what's most comfortable for you. (Note: this is one of the longest exercises in the book!)

Time Needed: **15 MINUTES**
Location: **A QUIET PLACE**

It may be helpful to close your eyes.

Take a deep breath.

Breathe in. Pause for a second. And now breathe out.

Notice how you are sitting. Is your body relaxed or tense?

Breathe in and think RELAX.

And breathe out again.

Imagine a time when you felt really happy. When you felt loved, full of energy, excited, but also peaceful. Perhaps it was at a birthday party or on the sports field or watching a movie with your family. Or maybe it was just a time when you were hanging out with friends. If it is hard for you to think of any time, then create a time. Think about where you would be and what kind of people would surround you.

Now, choose just one time. SEE where you are. Are you inside or outside? Who is around you? Do you remember what you were wearing? Or simply make up your outfit. Just see it in your head.

HEAR where you are. What sounds can you hear? Is there music on? Or is it quiet? Even in the quiet, can you hear sounds in nature or the everyday sounds of your school or house? Are people talking?

SMELL where you are. It may sound funny but try to focus on what it smells like. Maybe you remember the unique perfume your grandmother wears or you can smell the trees that surround you.

TASTE where you are. If you are eating something, imagine the taste of what makes you feel good. You may want to make up something that you love to eat if you can't taste anything right away.

Take another deep breath. In and out.

Now . . .

FEEL. How do you feel inside?

Put your attention on your heart and breathe in the feeling of PEACE.

Breathe in and out.

Take another breath, in and out, and tell yourself to remember this feeling.

Open your eyes if they were closed.

If you feel like it, you may want to write notes about or draw your feelings. What does your happy place feel like? If you had to draw the feelings, what would they look like? Sometimes it is helpful to look at these notes or drawings once a day. And, in those moments when you feel stressed, you can look at your notes or drawing or just close your eyes and see the images again.

What Your Breathing Tells You

· · · · ·

Breathing is nourishing to your body. When you breathe in, oxygen gives your cells the energy they need to keep you healthy. Breath stimulates movement and circulation.

As you breathe out, you release carbon dioxide and toxins (bad chemicals) from your body. Think about it: breathing is what tells you that you are actually alive!

Your thoughts are linked to your breath. When your mind is racing with thoughts, particularly when you get excited (happy or not so happy), your breathing usually gets faster. Think about when you are about to get on a roller coaster or enter a haunted house: do you feel like your breathing gets faster?

What about when you are really upset because your parents got mad at you or you had a fight with your best friend? In between cries, your breathing is usually faster, as well. Maybe you get so upset that it feels like your breath is too fast and you just can't slow down. And then, suddenly, you have to take a deep breath to calm down.

Or do you find your breathing growing faster when you feel you have too much homework or too many extracurricular things to do?

When you are overwhelmed, you start to experience that stressed, anxious feeling—almost like butterflies fluttering in your stomach.

Breathing on purpose can be one of the most helpful ways to get back in control of any situation. It can also help get you ready to face challenges, to take a pause and think before you act so that you make smart decisions that feel right to you. Your breath is always with you—a good friend indeed!

Just Breathe

· · · · ·

Right now, take a deep breath.

Breathe in.

And out.

Again.

Breathe in and out.

Do you notice that when you are breathing your mind stops racing? Try thinking a thought and breathing at the same time. For example, say your name in your mind and then breathe. You will notice that your mind jumps from thinking your name to noticing your breath. It is hard to do both at the same time!

In this way, breathing helps you control your racing thoughts. You can control what's going on in your head by changing how you breathe. When you are in control of your thoughts, you will act more calmly, will be more relaxed, and will generally find you are happier.

Breathe.

In.

Out.

Breathe again.

Think of your breath as an anchor. No matter what is happening around you, no matter how busy you are, no matter who surrounds you, you can always find your breath. It is a stable and secure part of you.

You breathe when you sleep and when you dream. You also breathe when you meditate. Breath is the life force that keeps your body and mind aware and healthy.

BREATHING MEDITATION

Just breathing is one of the most powerful ways for you to relax. Practicing breathing every day for two minutes is a good habit that will make your brain and body healthier, give you more energy, and make you happier.

Time Needed: **1 MINUTE**
Location: **ANYWHERE**

Find a comfortable, quiet place. You can do this meditation anywhere and at any time.

Turn off all devices and the television so that you are not distracted. This will last only one minute—you can do it!

Sit comfortably. If you feel okay doing so, close your eyes. If you prefer to keep your eyes open, that is okay, too.

Take a deep breath in through your nose. Breathe in deeply so that your lungs fill up.

As you breathe in, feel how your stomach goes out.

Pause for just one second.

And now breathe out, blowing out slowly from your mouth.

On your next breath in, try to breathe in for three seconds. One. Two. Three.

Now, pause for two seconds. One. Two.

And breathe out for four seconds. One. Two. Three. Four.

Find the rhythm that works best for you. Breathe in. Pause. Breathe out.

After one minute, or once you feel you are done, open your eyes (if they were closed) and say THANK YOU to yourself for giving your brain and body this experience.

If you do this meditation regularly, it will become a habit and it will become a safe, happy time for you. You can always find your breath no matter where you are.

Breathe

BLOW THOSE BUTTERFLIES AWAY

Do you ever get butterflies in your stomach? It's that fluttery, dizzying feeling inside you. Perhaps you feel them fly around the morning before the first day of school? Or when you are heading to a new summer camp where you don't know anyone. Or when your coach has just told you that after the next time-out, you are going to have to play those last few seconds of a tied game.

You feel your breath and heartbeat getting faster as you are both excited and nervous. But those butterflies just won't go away, no matter what.

Here's something you can do to help get that feeling to leave your stomach. You may want to try it a few times at home so when you need to do it in a nervous situation, you know how.

Time Needed: **LESS THAN A MINUTE**
Location: **ANYWHERE**

Notice where the butterflies are most crazy. Maybe they are making your head light. Or you feel them in your arms and head. Or your heart. Or stomach. Or all over!

Choose one area and actually think of colorful butterflies. Blue. Red. Yellow. Purple. Beautiful, colorful butterflies!

Now, take a deep breath through your nose.

Pause. And get ready to blow them away.

Then, BLOW those butterflies away by pushing your breath out from your mouth.

Try it again.

Find the butterflies.

Breathe in deep.

Pause and get ready to really blow them away.

Push your breath out from your mouth and imagine those beautiful, colorful butterflies flying far away!

FALLING ASLEEP

Sometimes it's hard to fall asleep. Your mind races with thoughts from the day, or you might be worried about something you need to do tomorrow.

Here is an exercise you can try before sleeping to help you get rid of all of those thoughts keeping you awake. It's best to try this exercise a few times even on a normal night to see how it makes you feel. If you have practiced it a few times, then when you need it to work, it will feel easy and natural!

Time Needed: **1 TO 2 MINUTES RIGHT BEFORE YOUR GO TO SLEEP**
Location: **IN YOUR BED**

Lie in bed on your back. Place a comfortable pillow under your head, and get cozy and tucked into your blanket or sheets.

Put one hand on your stomach and one above your heart.

Close your eyes, and take a natural breath in.

As you breathe in, feel your stomach rise.

Now, breathe out.

As you breathe out, feel how your lungs and the area around your heart settles down.

Try it once again.

Now, put your hands by your sides.

Take a breath in, slowly, in your head saying, "ONE. TWO. THREE."

And, as you breathe out, in your head, say, "ONE. TWO. THREE. FOUR."

ONE. TWO. THREE as you breathe in.

ONE. TWO. THREE. FOUR as you breathe out.

Do this ten times.

When you are done, just continue to breathe normally. Wish yourself sweet dreams and a good night's sleep.

If you find that you are still tossing and turning, start from the beginning and count ten breaths again. You may find it easier to change the count to **ONE** as you breathe in; **ONE-TWO** as you breathe out. Try it ten times and then breathe normally again.

HELP, I HAVE A HEADACHE!

Today, sadly, lots of kids get headaches. Headaches seem to come from a variety of factors: some are linked to stress, diet, lack of sleep, or dehydration. For some kids, they may come when your body is growing and going through lots of changes. And for some, unfortunately, they show up unexpectedly. You may have to learn to manage the pain and get through them as peacefully as possible.

Here are a few tips that may help prevent headaches:

> ° Sleep well—nine to ten hours at least!

> ° Exercise regularly—the yoga exercises in this book
> are great exercises, but you can also go for a run, play a sport,
> take a bike ride, or even jump rope!

> ° Notice if you get headaches when you eat
> certain foods or miss a meal.

> ° Drink lots of water.

If you do get a headache one day, though, try this meditation to relieve it:

Time Needed: **2 MINUTES**
Location: **A DARK ROOM**

When you have a bad headache, it may be more comfortable to sit in a dark, cool room.

Sit as comfortably as you can. If you feel more comfortable, you can lie down.

Place your hands in your lap or by your sides with your palms facing up.

Begin by breathing. Breathe in to the count of three. One. Two. Three.

Pause.

Then, breathe out to the count of four. One. Two. Three. Four.

Now, continue to breathe and put your attention on your heart. Can you feel your heart beat? Sense its rhythm?

Shift your attention to the tips of your fingertips. See if you can feel your heart beat in your fingers.

Take another deep breath in and out.

Stay as comfortable as you can, lying down, and nap, if possible.

The goal of this meditation is to help divert the blood flow from your brain to other parts of your body. When you get a headache, often the blood vessels in your head, neck, and shoulders get smaller. By feeling your heart beat in your fingers, you may help your blood flow better and improve your headache.

Breathe

A MEDITATION FOR PAIN

Breathing can help you deal with pain, like an upset stomach, sore ankle, or discomfort in your back. Breath brings oxygen into the body, and steady breathing helps you relax, which may alleviate some of your discomfort.

Time Needed: **ANY AMOUNT**
Location: **ANYWHERE**

Take a deep breath. Breathe in. One. Two. Three.

Pause.

Breathe out. One. Two. Three. Four.

As you breathe, realize that the oxygen you are breathing in helps you work better. Feel and see the healing energy of the air. Imagine the air as a cooling blue color. As you breathe in, see how the air, that blue color, travels through your body.

Put your attention on the area feeling pain. For example, if you are having a stomachache, put your attention on your tummy.

Now, let your breath come in and out from your stomach.

So, your stomach breathes in that blue, cooling, healing air. One. Two. Three.

As you pause, see the blue air spreading through the pain.

And, as you breathe out, see the pain leaving your body.

Let your body breathe in and out like this five to ten times, focusing on the area where you are feeling pain.

When you are ready, breathe deeply once again, in and out.

And continue your regular breathing.

Hopefully, you will feel some relief after doing this simple meditation! You can do this exercise regularly, focusing on different parts of your body as needed.

COOLING DOWN

When you get angry, or even embarrassed, do you ever notice that your body also heats up? Your face gets red, and you can feel the heat boiling inside of you. This is a very normal reaction when you are mad, upset, or feeling self-conscious.

The next breathing exercise may feel weird at first, but it is great for cooling down your temper or when you are feeling really hot inside. You can do this at any time, but it is worth trying once when you have a spare moment, so that when you need to do it for real, you know how!

Time Needed: **1 MINUTE**
Location: **ANYWHERE**

Open your mouth and curl your tongue, shaping it like a straw. (Some people can't curl their tongue. If you can't, just keep it flat in your mouth.)

Breathe in through your tongue, slurping in air like you would if it was your favorite drink.

Close your mouth and breathe out through your nose.

Let's do it again.

Open your mouth and curl your tongue. Breathe in.

Close your mouth. And breathe out from your nose.

You may notice that as you breathe in, the air feels cool, and as you breathe out, you let the heat from inside you escape through your nostrils.

Once you know how to do it, try it the next time you are upset. You don't have to make it obvious—just open your mouth a little, curl your tongue, and breathe in and out.

Breathe

BUMBLEBEE BREATH

When you are stressed and upset, sometimes it feels like your mind is buzzing inside. It may be that your thoughts are coming quickly and they can't seem to stop. Perhaps you have a hard time paying attention when someone else is speaking and it's difficult for you to focus on anything. You may even get headaches from all the agitation.

Letting that *buzz* out can help you feel more relaxed and let go of any type of stress.

Time Needed: **1 MINUTE**
Location: **ANYWHERE**

Put your pointer finger on the flap of your ear (the part that is between your cheek and the hole in your ear).

Test pushing those flaps into your ear so that you block the hole going to your eardrum. You may notice that perhaps you can hear a buzzing sound when you block out the external noise. Remove your fingers, opening the hole again.

Keep your earhole open as you take a deep breath in.

Pause, and with your fingers, push your earflaps down.

Hum as you breathe out gently from your mouth. Feel the vibration and the buzzing as it releases from your body. Continue for one minute and see if that buzzing hasn't stopped along with any stress you were feeling.

MOVE

Moving Is Good!

· · · · ·

Movement is healthy for your mind and your body.

When you move, you stretch your muscles, you breathe in air that nurtures your body, you sweat out toxins, and your brain releases chemicals that make you happy.

If you play sports, you probably know how great you feel after an intense game or scrimmage. Not only does your body feel full of energy (and perhaps a bit sore), but your mind also feels clear and happy!

You can move in different ways to get more energy or calm down to be more in control of how you feel throughout the day.

Walking Meditations

· · · · ·

Most of us walk every day. Perhaps you walk to school or take your dog for a walk in the evening. Or maybe you walk from one classroom to another after each class period. Or you might even go up the stairs to your bedroom each night and morning. Or perhaps you just like to walk around your neighborhood—by yourself, with friends, or with your family. If you are in a wheelchair, you probably have your own way of getting around that includes movement and a routine. Noticing how your mind and body work together effortlessly when you are doing something as routine as walking is a reminder about the magnificence of the human body.

Most of the time, you probably don't pay attention to how you are walking or moving. Sometimes you may take for granted where you walk and not notice what's around you. When you are no longer aware of your surroundings and how you interact with them, you can get lost in your own world. This can be unsafe but also isolating and boring!

In these two walking meditations, the goal is to reconnect with your body and your most basic movement and to become more aware of your surroundings.

A ROUTINE WALK IN A NEW WAY

- - - - - - - - - - - - -

Time Needed: **AS LONG AS YOU WANT**
Location: **A NORMAL WALK**

Let's choose a walk you do every day. The walk can be as simple as going from your kitchen to your bedroom or your daily walk to school. Plan to take the same time you normally do to make that walk happen then add a minute at the beginning and at the end.

For today's walk, you should plan on doing it without music and without talking (if you are planning on joining a parent, sibling, or friend). Today, when you walk, you are going to pay attention to your surroundings.

Before your start, stand still with your arms by your sides, close your eyes, and take a deep breath in and out.

Be aware of your posture before you move and make sure you stand tall. Does your body feel full of energy, or are you a little tired today? Note how you are feeling in this moment.

Tell yourself, "I am going to be aware of my surroundings on this walk."

Open your eyes, and before you start, take a moment to look around you. Observe what your surroundings are.

Choose ten things you see and say their names to yourself.

Smell the odors—good and bad—and try to figure out where they are coming from.

Listen to the sounds around you. What is creating those sounds? Take a moment to listen to the quieter sounds as well as the loud sounds.

Feel how hot or cold it is. Is there a breeze or is it still where you are? Is the sun shining on you or is it perhaps moist or raining?

If you are inside, what is the light like? Do you have sunlight coming through the window or are the light bulbs on?

Now, it's time to go. Lift up one foot and begin walking.

As you walk, at your normal pace, pay attention to your surroundings.

Look around you. See if you can notice something you haven't seen before.

Breathe.

MOVE

With each breath, notice how the air is entering your lungs—is it cool or warm?

Notice the smells around you.

Listen. Are the sounds changing as you move?

Once you have arrived at your destination, take another moment to close your eyes and breathe a deep breath in and out.

Think about any new things you may have noticed during this walk. Sometimes a walk like this can make an old place look brand-new.

Did it feel different taking this walk when you were quiet and noticing? Were you more aware of your muscles and how your body works? Did you notice anything that you hadn't seen before, even though you do this same walk every day?

A mindful walk helps you connect with your body and appreciate how many things come together when you move. You may realize that you aren't feeling so great today and need more rest or something to eat. This is an opportunity to see your everyday world with a fresh perspective. Perhaps a new adventure awaits you!

MOVE

A REAL SLOW AND QUIET WALK

In this exercise, you are going to notice how you walk. It's a real slow walk that can help you slow down when life seems a bit too fast. Let's begin with ten steps and then you can always increase it over time.

Time Needed: **1 MINUTE**
Location: **ANYWHERE**

Before you do anything, notice your posture. Do you stand straight, or do your slouch a bit? Be sure you stand tall for this exercise.

Notice where your arms are. Do you fold them in front of you or put your hands in your pockets? Let your arms hang relaxed by your sides.

Let your eyes look ahead. It may be easier to focus on something in the distance.

With each step, you are going to take a breath, in and out. Then pause. And then take another step.

Step One: As you lift your foot, breathe in, and as you place it down, breathe out.

Pause.

Step Two: Breathe in as you lift your foot; breathe out as you put it down.

Repeat until you have taken ten steps. (It may help to count inside your head as you do this, like so:

One as you breathe in and out.

Two as you breathe in and out.

Three as you breathe in and out.

Continue until you reach ten.)

Now, count to ten in your head before you end the exercise. Let your breathing go back to normal and think about what it felt like to walk slowly. Did you feel different? Were you more aware of how your muscles worked together to transport you?

WHAT IS YOGA?

Yoga is a way for you to connect your body, your mind, and your breath.

Yoga helps your body get rid of stress by releasing toxins (bad chemicals), by stretching, by getting more flexible and stronger, and by building up the good hormones in your bodies that can make you happier and healthier.

Yoga is different from exercise in gym class or in extracurricular sports, which are also very important and good for you! Yoga, however, is slower and focuses more on breathing and stretching to help your body recover from stress and to grow stronger.

Yoga Poses

· · · · ·

Many different poses in yoga can be combined to create a practice that is comfortable for you. For some, yoga is a way to stretch; for others, yoga is a way to increase blood flow, build stamina, or gain flexibility. You can choose how fast or slow you go in yoga, and you can create a routine that works for you. There are certain "flows" in yoga—combinations of set poses—that focus on connecting to your entire body. In this book, you will learn the very basics to give you a taste of yoga.

While yoga involves movement, let's begin with just standing tall and still!

MOUNTAIN

A mountain is strong, stable, grand, and unmovable. By standing tall like a mountain, you can feel more in control of your body—and more in control of your world. You'll soon feel strong and stable in the midst of the chaos and stress around you.

1. Stand tall with your arms hanging by your sides and your hands loose (not closed into fists).

2. Keep your feet apart and totally flat on the ground.

3. Look straight ahead with your head standing tall.

4. Imagine a light string pulling your head up into the sky.

5. Breathe in and out.

6. Imagine you're a snow-capped mountain—taller than everyone else—the strong protector of all the lands that surround you. The clouds come and go around you, but you still stand tall. Perhaps you can see the rains below you, but you remain grounded and stable.

7. Breathe in and out. In and out.

Try breathing in and out five times the first time you do this, and then see if you can get to ten or even twenty breaths!

TREE

Do you ever feel like you have too many things happening at once during the day? Do you feel that you just go from one activity to another, or that you feel tired, but don't have time to rest?

Learning how to find balance when you are young can help you as you get older and have more and more responsibilities.

This pose is a nice way to physically focus on balance. You may notice that you have to calm your mind to settle your body and be able to balance in this pose.

1. Start in Mountain Pose, standing tall and strong.

2. Take a deep breath. Pay attention to how you are standing. Your shoulders should be straight, arms by your sides, and feet planted firmly on the ground.

3. Breathe in and out, slowly and deeply.

4. With your left foot staying on the ground, focus on your feet as an anchor. You can keep your left leg straight or, if it's more comfortable, bend it just a bit.

5. With a breath, in and out, bring your hands together, palms facing each other like you are praying.

6. As you take your next breath in, begin to lift your right foot and keep balancing on your left leg. First, just put your right foot by your left ankle. Keep balancing. You may find yourself wavering from side to side. Think of yourself as a tree blowing in the wind but try to stand tall. You may find it is helpful to focus on one spot in front of you. You can exhale your breath as you find a comfortable pose.

7. Use your breath, in and out, to help you balance and stand tall. As you sway, refocus and breathe.

8. If you are balancing well, see if you can lift your right foot up your leg until you can place it right above the inside of your knee.

9. Breathe in and out.

10. Take a deep breath in, and as you exhale slowly, put your right foot down and lower your arms back to your sides.

11. Stand tall again, breathing in and out.

Let's do the other side:

1. Keep your right foot on the ground. Keep your hands by your side and anchor your feet to the ground.

2. Breathe in and out.

3. As you breathe in, lift your left foot and put it by the inside of your right ankle. Exhale as you find a comfortable position. Try to balance and if you have to put your foot down, let it down, take a breath, and try again.

4. If you can, lift your left foot to the inside of your right knee. Take a moment to balance. Again, use your breath to help you balance and find stability.

5. Breathe in and out. And then, slowly, put your left foot on the ground. Drop your hands to your sides.

6. Breathe in and out.

7. Stand again in Mountain Pose, and take one last breath, in and out.

DOWNWARD-FACING DOG

Have you ever noticed how a dog stretches when it wakes up from a nap? It leans forward with its front paws outstretched, lengthening its shoulders, neck, back, and hind legs. Its butt is usually up, pointing toward the sky, too.

When you do this pose, you can stretch your body and get more energy for your day. It's a good pose to wake up with or even to do when you need a boost of energy.

1. Start by standing tall in Mountain Pose.

2. Take a deep breath in and out.

3. Move to the ground, balancing on your hand and knees, with your back flat like you are a table.

4. Reach your arms out in front of you and put your hands flat on the ground.

5. Take a deep breath in and out.

6. Now, push your hands to the ground and straighten your legs. Let your head hang straight down between your arms. Feel the stretch in the back of your legs and through your arms.

7. Take another deep breath, in and out.

8. Bend your knees back to the ground. Bring your hands back in front of you so that you are again like a table. Breathe in and out.

9. Then, stand up again in Mountain Pose. Breathe in and out.

MOVE

CAT AND COW

Have you ever seen how a cat stretches its back—arching its back up to the sky and releasing all the tension inside? Have you ever wondered how a cow stretches with its long body?

    This yoga pose is good for stretching your spine. Think of it like giving yourself a massage inside.

1. Begin with your hands and knees on the ground and your back flat like a table.

2. Let your head relax. Your eyes can look at the ground between your hands.

3. Take a deep breath in and out. First, you will stretch like a cat.

4. Taking a deep breath in, lift your back to the ceiling, like you are making an arch so that someone can crawl under you. Let your head naturally follow the arch, looking at the floor.

5. While breathing out, come back to the tabletop position with your back flat. Now stretch in the opposite direction.

6. Taking a deep breath in, lift your head and butt to the ceiling. Imagine you are creating a stretched-out U at the bottom of your back that could hold some water. Your eyes can look up to the ceiling.

7. While breathing out, come back to the tabletop position.

8. Take a deep breath in and out.

9. Repeat both poses again.

10. When you are done, return to the tabletop position, and breathe in and out before coming out of the pose.

COBRA

A cobra is a snake that has a lot of power. It slithers on the ground, and when it is ready to attack, it raises its head high and proud, then strikes quickly. It is focused and strong.

This pose helps you stretch your back, neck, and shoulders—areas where you can hold stress in your body. If you get headaches, this may be one to try on a regular basis. The main point to remember with this exercise is to be gentle. Think of the snake slithering: it does so smoothly and without much effort.

1. Lie on your stomach. Let your legs stretch out long behind you and your feet point toward the back of the room.

2. Breathe in and out. Think of the power that comes with the pause between your breaths. Breathe in, pause, and breathe out.

3. Bend your elbows and put your hands by the side of your shoulders.

4. Now, as you breathe in, gently straighten your arms, lifting your head and looking straight ahead. Don't stretch too far; rather, put your energy into focusing on something ahead of you.

5. Count to ten, breathing in and out at a pace that is comfortable for you. If you prefer counting to three at first, that is okay.

6. Take another breath in, and as you breathe out, gently come back down, bending your arms.

7. Put your arms by your sides to rest for a few seconds. You can turn your head to one side if that is comfortable.

8. Breathe in and out at least two times to rest.

BUTTERFLY

After a long day of sitting at school or at home, sometimes you just need to stretch your muscles to release tension.

If you get pain in your stomach (maybe trouble going to the bathroom) and abdominal area (maybe cramps from your period, if you are a girl), this exercise can help release tension to make you feel better.

1. Sit on the ground and spread your legs in a V in front of you.

2. Bring your feet together, creating a diamond. Your two feet should be facing each other and touching. Bring your feet as close to your body as possible. You can use your hands to hold your feet to keep your balance.

3. Take three deep breaths in and out.

4. Now, keeping your feet together, breathe out and push your knees and thighs down toward the floor. No need to force them—just let your knees go down as much as is comfortable.

5. And now lift your legs up as you breathe in.

6. Move your knees up and down several times, breathing out as you push your knees down and breathing in as you let them come back up. Think of your legs as the wings of a butterfly flapping up and down.

7. After five to ten flaps, you may want to try bending your face to the ground and see how it feels. You may get a nice stretch in your lower back and feel more release in your legs. Only do what is comfortable.

8. Once you are done, straighten your legs.

9. Take a deep breath in and out.

HAPPY BABY

Think of a baby, cooing, laughing, and rolling around on the ground. Everything seems new and magical, maybe even a little confusing and scary, as a new little person. One minute the baby is nervous and crying, but a second later she is smiling again.

Do you remember what it felt like to be a baby with no worries in the world?

When you do this next pose, imagine you are a baby, letting go of all your stress, your to-do lists, and your emotional hurts.

1. Lie on your back and bend your legs. Imagine your knees bending toward your ears.

2. Straighten your arms on the inside of your legs by your knees, and hold the bottoms of your feet. Your left hand should be holding your left foot, and your right hand should be holding your right foot. If you can't reach your feet, you can put your hands on the outside of your knees.

3. Take a deep breath in and out.

4. Now, as you breathe in, pull your feet toward you, bending your knees and feeling the stretch in your butt. Be gentle, but notice how you can massage your lower back by moving your feet slightly. Exhale your breath comfortably.

5. Smile, and feel like a baby. Maybe try rolling a little from side to side and have fun. Continue to breathe in and out.

6. When you are done, lie down again on your back for a few seconds before sitting up.

7. Breathe in and out consciously, turn to your side, and when comfortable, sit up.

MOVE

BE STILL

Sometimes lying down without doing anything can be the most relaxing or most difficult thing to do.

In yoga, you activate your muscles, increase your heart rate, breathe more deeply, and raise your body temperature. Lying down for a few minutes at the end is important for bringing your body back to normal.

Being still after movement also lets your mind and body appreciate the benefits of the practice. In this silent, still time after movement, you can note what changes may have taken place and feel the good hormones flowing through your body with each breath. Savor the good feelings, and try to carry them with you throughout your day!

1. Lie down on your back. Your hands and arms should be by your side and your legs straight out and feet relaxed.

2. Close your eyes.

3. And just be still. And silent. And notice how your body feels.

4. Breathe in and out. In and out. In and out.

5. And do nothing.

6. Your mind may wander here and there, to noises around you or to remembering things that happened earlier in the day or yesterday or two years ago! When you notice you are daydreaming, just breathe again and notice how your body is feeling.

7. Take three more breaths. In and out. In and out. In and out.

8. Open your eyes.

9. When you feel ready, you can turn to one side and sit up.

After doing yoga poses, it is always a good idea to take a moment to "wake up." Sometimes you daydream while doing yoga, and your mind wanders. This can be wonderful and relaxing. But, when it is time to return to the day's activities, you want to be present and aware of what's happening around you.

The benefits of yoga, breathing, meditation, and mindfulness are felt in your daily activities. With practice, you should feel calmer, focus easier, and generally be happier during your everyday routines.

Yoga Flow

· · · · ·

To begin yoga, practice each of the poses outlined on the previous page. As you get more comfortable, you may enjoy combining them and creating your own routine, or yoga flow!

Here are a few combinations of the poses that you may find fun to do:

- Mountain Pose – Tree Pose – Mountain Pose
- Mountain Pose – Downward Dog – Mountain Pose – Be Still
- Downward Dog – Cat and Cow Pose – Downward Dog – Be Still
- Downward Dog – Cobra – Cat and Cow Pose – Downward Dog – Be Still
- Downward Dog – Butterfly – Happy Baby – Be Still
- Mountain Pose – Tree Pose – Mountain Pose – Downward Dog –
  Cobra – Cat and Cow Pose – Downward Dog –
  Butterfly – Happy Baby – Be Still

If you like these, you can read more about yoga, watch some YouTube videos, or ask your parents or a caretaker to take you to a yoga class.

The Sounds around Me

·····

Sounds have the incredible power to affect your mood. When there is a lot of commotion around you, it is hard to focus and feel at peace. And, sometimes when it is too quiet, perhaps you feel restless and bored.

Think of the beat of drums. Depending on how fast or slow the beat is, you may want to dance or you may find yourself falling into a trance. Does the sound of a flute make you feel different from the sound of a trumpet?

Think of some peaceful, quiet sounds that make you feel relaxed.

Often, people find that nature sounds make them feel restful—the sounds of waves, the chirping of birds, or the wind blowing through trees. These sounds often have a rhythm or vibration that is soothing to you.

Perhaps you have some favorite music that makes you feel happy and peaceful—a classical piece of piano music or a creative jazz piece that lets your mind wander and get lost. Or maybe your prayers from your church, temple, or mosque are the most soothing and peaceful sounds for you.

Depending on your mood, you can choose to have happy, energetic, peaceful, or healing sounds around you. It may be helpful to keep notes about sounds you like and how they make you feel. If there is a song on the radio that makes you feel like dancing with joy, write down the title so you can play it the next time you need a pick-me-up. If there is a family prayer that helps you feel connected to your world, find that the next time you feel lonely. Having a playlist of sounds that supports you can be one of your greatest companions.

The Power of Silence

• • • • •

One of the most powerful, peaceful, and safe places can be found right inside of you.

You might feel that silence can make you feel lonely, confused, or scared. But that is often because being quiet is something you are not used to.

You live in a world that constantly has noise and distractions: voices, traffic, machines, music, television, opinions, and social media. The only time you get some quiet is at night, hopefully, when you sleep. And that is when your body and mind rest.

Giving your mind quiet time throughout the day is healthy for your brain and your body. Quiet time actually changes your brain so that you can focus better, see things more positively, and not be so tired and reactive to everything.

When you are quiet, you can honestly ask yourself questions about what you want and who you want to be. You can take away everyone's opinions and the social pressures about who you should be, and listen to yourself. You know deep inside what is best for *you*. In that quiet space, you can learn to trust yourself. And in that silence, you can think about how to get the life you want to live.

I AM

- -

Your mind might feel like it's racing most of the time. One thought makes you have another thought, which leads you to yet *another* thought. Here's an example of how this vicious cycle might go:

I am hungry.

I want an ice cream.

Where will I get it from?

I can ask my mom if we can go to my favorite ice cream place.

But I may see those friends there who were getting together and didn't invite me.

Why didn't they invite me?

What's wrong with me?

You can see how one simple thought can take you down a path of lots of other thoughts—some a little deeper than just wanting some ice cream. And often you could end up thinking thoughts that aren't even true but that make you feel insecure, anxious, or unhappy.

When you slow down your thoughts, you can get better at not letting yourself get carried away by your imagination or worries. Here is an exercise you can try to help slow down your thoughts and keep more in the moment.

Time Needed: **5 MINUTES**
Location: **A QUIET PLACE**

Just Breathe

Find a comfortable place. Shut off the television or video games. If you have an electronic device like a phone or an iPad, put it away or on silent mode.

It will be nice if you can close your eyes, but you don't have to. Also, don't worry about the time you give to this exercise. You can estimate five minutes or use a clock to help with the time.

Take a deep breath. IN and OUT.

In your head, think the words, I AM.

And keep repeating them: I AM. I AM. I AM.

You can repeat the words slowly or quickly—whatever pace is most comfortable for you. Just keep repeating I AM.

After a couple of repetitions, your mind will begin to wander. You may remember the homework assignment you forgot to do. Or think about your upcoming soccer game. Or start replaying something your friend said this morning that hurt you.

Wherever your mind wanders, just decide that for right now, you are only going to repeat I AM.

I AM. I AM. I AM.

You may find that the words now speed up or slow down. Let the words do whatever they want to do. Just keep repeating them.

Don't forget to breathe naturally and repeat I AM. I AM. I AM.

When you are ready to be done, stop repeating I AM. Take a deep breath in and out. Open your eyes.

How did this meditation feel? Did you feel like your mind settled down or did the phrase I AM lead you to think more thoughts? The interesting thing about this meditation (and many others in this book) is that each time you try it, you may have a different experience. Maybe this time, the I AMs came really fast at first, but you got distracted and forgot to repeat them. Or maybe they were really slow and then you fell asleep. Or maybe you were focused on saying I AM and the words automatically came and you drifted away. *All* of these experiences are normal and natural. Your mind will react with each meditation in the way that it needs to in that moment. If you fall asleep, it means you need more rest; if your mind races with thoughts, it's a sign that maybe you are trying to do too many things; if you find it easy to repeat the words and you drift away, then your mind will get rest.

FIND YOUR WORD

You may have a favorite word or feeling that you can use for your regular meditation practice.

In the earlier exercise, you tried repeating I AM, but maybe another word or phrase makes you feel confident and inspired that you would like to try. Or perhaps a sound makes you feel calm and relaxed that you can use the next time you meditate.

Different words, phrases, and sounds can create different feelings inside and can make you feel different levels of calm. Here are some ideas of words and phrases you could try:

Love	*Laughter*	*I Am Loved*
Peace	*Harmony*	*I Love*
Happy	*Power*	*I See*
Wisdom	*I Can*	

You could also choose a phrase from any prayers or religion you might have that makes you feel peaceful and relaxed. Really, the sky's the limit!

Time Needed: **5 MINUTES**
Location: **ANYWHERE**

Sit comfortably. If you are comfortable, close your eyes.

Begin with two deep breaths. In and out. In and out.

Repeat your word or phrase. You can say it at a pace that is comfortable for you.

When your attention drifts away, just focus on your word or phrase again.

Notice that your breath may slow down and that you feel more relaxed. You may also start to feel sleepy. Or your mind may race to other thoughts, no matter how many times you try to bring it back to your word, phrase, or sound.

No matter where your mind wanders, when you notice it doing that, just repeat your word again.

When the time is up, take a deep breath and stop repeating your word or phrase. Open your eyes.

A QUIET MEAL

Do you ever find that mealtimes have become busy and distracted? Whether the distraction is TV, YouTube, social media, or a busy household, even eating can feel chaotic!

Appreciating your food is a magical and fun experience that you can do with your family or friends. Foods offer so many flavors—sweet, sour, salty, bitter. Food has different textures from smooth to crunchy, and it can taste different depending on its temperature. Rather than just seeing your food as the fuel to keep you alive, take the time to savor your bites and you may discover how interesting and entertaining food can be.

Here is an exercise you can try with your family.

Time Needed: **5 TO 10 MINUTES**
Location: **AT A MEAL**

Choose a meal—say, dinner—and decide that everyone sitting at the table will spend five to ten minutes eating quietly. That means no TV, no cell phones, and no talking.

Everyone will fill their plate, and then you will time ten minutes for everyone to look, feel, smell, taste, and eat their food.

Notice the colors of your food.

Smell the food and, with each bite, note the flavors.

Really try to eat your meal without talking. See if it feels awkward or natural.

When you are ready, go around the table and discuss how the experience felt for everyone.

Eating your meal in silence will heighten your other senses to appreciate the food you're eating. You may also notice, during the silent time, how you normally take the food you eat for granted. Doing this exercise with your family will be a nice way for you to connect—perhaps you all will realize that being distracted takes away from the meal and the special time you have to connect. You may also notice how you can be together, even if you aren't talking.

Disconnect, Please?

• • • • •

Sometimes, TV helps you relax and live in a fantasy world. Social media helps you connect with friends and family. Video games allow you to be creative and pass the time. When not overdone, media can make your life more interesting and fun.

But TV, video games, and social media can also trick your mind. They can stimulate you to feel happy and connected in not so healthy ways. Media can be used to escape your problems and the world—but when you do this, you often find that problems get worse or you feel more isolated from others. Sometimes watching too much TV can come at the cost of not exercising and enjoying the outdoors. Video games can be fun, but they can also be addictive and make violence seem normal. Social media can make you feel like you have been left out of fun events or that you have fewer friends or a more boring life than others. You can get lost in your devices, not even realizing that time is slipping away. Before you know it, you don't have time to do your homework or are always tired.

Finding a balance in your media habits will help you in life because you are probably only going to have more emails, more texts, more Snapchats, more Instagram likes, and so on as you get older. And ask your parents or anyone who is older than you—it is easy to get lost in media.

Here are a few tips on how you can find more balance and be more mindful about how you use social media and other forms of online or TV entertainment:

- Limit how much time you spend watching TV or playing video games. Agree to the amount of time with your parents. Impress them by taking responsibility and setting the rules together—and following them!

- Set aside time to check your phone or computer for social media, emails, or texts each day. But make sure you aren't checking constantly throughout the day.

- When you check your email or social media, check and respond. Choose two to three times when you check these things, but otherwise keep your devices away from you or turned off.

- Put your phone away and close your computer when you are doing homework. If you have to be online while doing homework, close any chat boxes or browsers that you don't need open for your schoolwork.

- If you have your computer open or your phone right next to you all the time, then every time it beeps you will be tempted to check it. Be sure to silence your phone and turn off any alerts so you aren't constantly glued to the screen, worrying that you'll be missing something or that you have to respond to text, or emails instantly.

By putting devices away, you will find you are more disciplined and less distracted by all the messages coming at you!

Be Silent

THE CLOUDS IN THE SKY

Sometimes life can feel overwhelming. Your mind may be racing with thoughts. You may feel excited one minute and sad the next. You may be confused or feel alone or feel too much pressure from other people.

When your life feels overwhelming, sometimes it can be helpful to remember that you are part of a larger universe. While you have problems that can seem unique and momentous, others have had similar problems and have also solved them. Just like the clouds in the sky come and go, so, too, do the problems and insecurities that will float in and out of your life. If you have faith that beyond the clouds of your mind there is a peaceful, blue sky, then you will know that every-thing will be okay.

You can do this next exercise whether you live in a city or the countryside—all it involves is looking up at the sky.

Time Needed: **5 MINUTES**
Location: **A COMFORTABLE PLACE OUTSIDE**

For this exercise, you need a blanket and to find a safe place outside, where you can lie on the ground. You should choose a time when the sun is not too bright (perhaps in the evening or even on a cloudy day). Take your time to find the right place. It may be in your backyard or at a park near your house. If you are doing this in a public place, ask your parents or a friend to go with you.

Lay the blanket on the ground. Lie on top of the blanket with your face toward the sky.

Close your eyes, and take a deep breath. In and out. Enjoy the feeling of being relaxed.

When you are ready, open your eyes, and look up into the sky. Feel how much space is between you and the sky. Does the sky end? Can you imagine space, stars, and galaxies continuing up, up, up beyond anything you can see?

Are there clouds? Do they look like cotton balls, or are they dark? Perhaps it looks like it might rain? Observe how the clouds move—slow or fast—across the sky.

They change shape and form, even color. Sometimes the sky looks blue, sometimes it is full of clouds.

Take a moment and note how this is similar to the thoughts in your head. Sometimes the thoughts—just like clouds—are so busy in your head. Sometimes they move quickly; other times more slowly. But just like the clouds in the sky, they move and change shape; they come and go.

But the sky continues to just be, reaching out endlessly into the universe.

Keep looking up and out at the endlessness of the sky.

When you feel ready, close your eyes again and take a deep breath.

The next time you feel overwhelmed with thoughts or have too many things to do, remember how it felt to look up at the sky. Remember the clouds coming and going.

And if it helps, maybe go outside and just look up at the sky again. It will always be there for you.

BEING ALONE

Are you ever in a crowd of people, yet feel like the loneliest person in the world? Do you ever feel this way even when you are with your close friends or family? Do you sometimes find yourself home alone, bored, like you have no one you can talk to or share experiences with?

Loneliness is different from being alone. Loneliness is when you feel sad and disconnected. When you are lonely, you should reach out to friends and loved ones. Being alone, however, can sometimes be filled with happiness and adventure. When you read a book, you are most often alone, but can enter a fantasy world filled with magic. When you sleep, you drift off into a world where you are alone but still have action around you.

If you learn to be comfortable with yourself, then you won't fear being alone. You will know that there are many fun and entertaining things you can do by yourself. You can draw, read, go for a walk, or dance to music that only you can hear. You can make up stories, do puzzles, or spend time researching a topic that no one else cares about.

Once you are comfortable being alone, you will also be more sensitive to when you actually feel sad and lonely and need to do something about it. You will know when it is time to reach out to others for some company. Sometimes, it just takes a few moments to remember that you are part of something—your family, your school community, your neighborhood, and your world.

Here is a meditation you can do when you feel lonely:

Time Needed: **2 MINUTES**
Location: **ANYWHERE**

Sit in a place where you feel comfortable. Choose a room that has a lot of light where you can even hear the sounds of your neighbors or people who are busily doing things.

If you are comfortable, close your eyes.

Put your attention on your heart: and say the following to yourself:

> *"I am part of something bigger than just me.*
>
> *I am part of something bigger than just me.*
>
> *I am part of a family.*
>
> *I am part of a community.*
>
> *I am part of this planet.*
>
> *I am.*
>
> *I am."*

With your attention on your heart, think of one thing you could do that would make another person happy. Maybe it is writing a letter to them or calling that distant relative or friend. What would make another person smile just now?

Take a deep breath, and open your eyes.

Make a plan to take action on that thing you can do to connect to someone else to make them happy. You may just find that it helps you feel connected and happy, too!

A MEDITATION FOR THE PLANET

- - - - - - - - - -

Our planet is often referred to as Mother Earth. She provides us with food, water, and the materials we use to protect ourselves. She gives us rainbows, sunsets, and places that take our breath away by her beauty.

When you feel connected to Mother Earth, then you are grounded—and you know you are connected to something magnificent!

Here is a meditation that may help you feel more connected to the planet.

Time Needed: **5 MINUTES**
Location: **A SAFE PLACE OUTSIDE**

Find a place in a park or out in nature where you feel safe and happy.

Sit comfortably.

Take a deep breath.

As you breathe in the air, thank Mother Earth for providing you the oxygen that keeps you alive and full of energy. As you breathe out, think about how lucky you are to live on this magnificent planet.

Think about Planet Earth's body—the mountains and valleys; the ground beneath your feet.

Think about the trees. Like our lungs, the trees breathe in and out.

Think about the streams and rivers. Like our blood, they circulate water and refresh the body.

Imagine the sounds of the waves of the ocean: the rise and fall as the wave approaches the shore; the consistent rhythm just like your heartbeat.

Feel the air around you. Whether it is warm or cold, the air provides you with energy and life force.

Feel the sun on your skin, how it warms and nurtures you, consistently, every day, even if hidden by the clouds.

Imagine raindrops falling on you. They are wiping away the dust and stresses of the day.

Look around you once again and soak in all Mother Earth has to offer.

Know and feel the earth, just as you feel the beat of your own heart.

KINDNESS FOR YOURSELF AND OTHERS

- - - - - - - - - - - - - - -

Most of us want to be loving and kind people. We also want people to treat us with love and kindness.

Sometimes, though, you might forget to be kind to yourself. It is natural. It is easy to criticize yourself because you know who you are better than anyone. You know your weaknesses and your insecurities, even if you are doing a good job hiding them from the rest of the world.

You may be trying to prove to the world that you are stronger, smarter, or more popular than you really feel. But if you remind yourself what's most important, if you are compassionate with yourself, then it is easier to be kind to others. Then, you'll also be more understanding of why people may not always be kind to you.

People find happiness and connection through love and kindness, so don't forget that you also have to have love and kindness for yourself, too.

This exercise, which comes from the Buddhist tradition in Asia, is meant to help you feel kind to yourself and others.

Time Needed: **15 MINUTES**

Location: **A QUIET AREA WHERE YOU CAN SPEAK OUT LOUD**

Sit comfortably.

Take a deep breath in and out to begin.

Continue breathing, and put your hand on your heart. Feel your heart take in energy as you breathe in. Imagine your heart releasing any hurt or stress as you breathe out.

With your hand on your heart, say the following phrases out loud:

> *"May I be safe and healthy.*
>
> *May I feel loved.*
>
> *May I be happy.*
>
> *May I feel at peace."*

Think of someone you love very much. Perhaps it is a parent or grandparent, a sibling, a friend, or a mentor who loves you no matter what.

Imagine that person sitting in front of you.

With your hand on your heart, say the following phrases out loud:

> *"May you be safe and healthy.*
>
> *May you feel loved.*
>
> *May you be happy.*
>
> *May you be at peace."*

Think of someone you know, but perhaps not so well (like the mail person or someone who works in a local store). Imagine that person in the place you normally see them.

With your hand still on your heart, say:

> *"May you be safe and healthy.*
>
> *May you feel loved.*
>
> *May you be happy.*
>
> *May you be at peace."*

And now think about all the people, animals, trees, and living things in this world. With true love in your heart, stretch your arms out and repeat these phrases:

> *"May you be safe and healthy.*
>
> *May you feel loved.*
>
> *May you be happy.*
>
> *May you be at peace."*

Take another deep breath in and out.

The Power of Noticing

• • • • •

Most of us are on the move all the time. Whether you are studying, playing, talking, reading, running, or working, you just keep going and going and going.

And when you fall asleep at night, you hopefully give your body a rest. But if you were able to give your body and mind some rest during the day, too, you could do *everything* you do more relaxed and easily.

This is where the idea of mindfulness comes in. Mindfulness means being aware of what's happening in your body, mind, and surroundings.

When you give your body and mind time to be quiet and do nothing, you will notice the amazing things that are happening inside and around you. When you are aware, you'll feel calmer. You'll make better decisions. You'll waste less energy worrying about things that don't really matter. And you may just find new, easier, and better ways of doing everyday things.

WHAT'S HAPPENING BOTH INSIDE AND OUTSIDE?

Conscious breathing exercises help you slow down, connect, and bring balance to your body. You will feel more in control when things may feel out of control. Noticing what's happening inside and around you is another powerful and easy way to help your body and your brain. It doesn't require much except your decision to be present and notice both what's going on inside your body and outside in the world.

Time Needed: **5 MINUTES**
Location: **ANYWHERE**

Sit comfortably—maybe on your bed, in your favorite chair, on cushions on the floor, or under a tree outside.

Close your eyes, and take a deep breath. In and out.

Notice the noises around you. Maybe you can hear your sibling or parent doing something in another room or the sound of your clock ticking or a machine buzzing or cars whizzing down the street.

As you hear the noises, you can label them: My sister. A car. My clock.

Breathe in and out.

Notice how, you, the one who is listening, are different from the noises you are hearing.

Take a deep breath and focus on what's going on inside of you instead of what's going on outside.

When you breathe in, feel your lungs go up and down.

Can you hear your heart beat? Do you see anything with your eyes closed? Do you hear your thoughts?

When you think a thought, label it: "That is a thought."

Take another breath in and out.

When you are ready, open your eyes.

There will always be distractions around you, but they come and go, and you don't need to be overwhelmed by them. Thoughts also come and go.

You can find a place inside you that stays stable through life's chaos. Your breath is always there to catch you and your heartbeat will keep the rhythm of your life at the pace you want it to be. Just trust yourself.

BE AWARE
OF YOUR BODY

Your body can tell you a lot about your feelings and your health. You may notice that when you have an upcoming test or a big competition, your stomach feels uneasy. Or you feel tension in your shoulders. Or you may find that when going to your new class for the first time or having to speak in front of your class, your heart beats faster and you start to sweat.

By noticing how your body reacts to certain situations, you can figure out ways to calm down when it feels like your body is taking over.

The first step is just becoming aware of your body, especially when you are calm. Here is a way you can start becoming aware of your body that should help you when you begin to feel tense or stressed.

Time Needed: **10 MINUTES**

Location: **A QUIET PLACE WITH ROOM TO LIE DOWN**

Find a comfortable place and lie down.

Close your eyes. If you fall asleep while doing this exercise, it is okay. It means that you are tired and your body needs more rest! But, instead of trying to fall asleep, you should try to notice different parts of your body.

Take a deep breath in and out. Again. In and out.

Put your attention on your toes. Curl them tight, then stretch them out. Take a deep breath, and imagine your toes breathing in the air and then letting it out.

Move your attention to your feet and ankles. Move them back and forth a bit, then turn them in a circle one way and then the other.

Put your attention on your calves and move up to your knees. You may want to bend your legs and stretch them out—feel your knees as you breathe in and out.

Move your awareness into your upper legs and to your pelvic area. Can you feel the air as you breathe in and out where your legs meet your body in the area below your stomach?

Put your attention on your stomach and take two deep breaths. Breathe in and out. In and out. Notice how your stomach rises a bit when you breathe in. And when you breathe out, it goes back down.

Move your attention to your heart. Can you feel your heart beat? Be still. Can you feel it? Breathe in and out.

Next focus your attention on your neck and shoulders. Move your head from side to side. Look left then right. Do it again.

Bring your attention to your hands. Bend your fingers into a tight fist then let go, stretching them wide. Breathe in and out. Imagine your fingers breathing in air, and then releasing it as you allow them to relax.

Move your attention up your elbows, bending them and straightening them out again. Breathe in and out.

Finally, come back to your neck and shoulders. Move your head left and right. Left and right again. Breathe in and out.

Now, let's pay attention to the way in which you process the world.

Put your attention on your tongue. Move it around in your mouth and run it over your teeth.

Open your mouth and breathe air in, pause, and let the air out.

Close your mouth and take your next breath through your nose. Breathe in and out. In and out. Feel the air go into your nostrils then to your lungs.

Move your attention to your closed eyes. Keeping them closed, just feel what it's like for your eyes to be taking a rest. Do you see anything with your eyes closed?

Breathe in and out.

Put your attention on your ears. What are they hearing right now as you breathe in and out?

Bring your attention to the space between your eyebrows. Breathe in and out.

Move your attention to the top of your head. Imagine the space above your head as your breathe in and out. In and out.

Now, see if you can pay attention to your whole body as you take one last deep breath in and out.

Open your eyes. Before you get up, say THANK YOU to your body. Appreciate how it serves you every day as you experience the world.

NOTICE WHAT YOU ARE EATING

You eat food to nurture your brain and your body, and to get energy so you can be active during the day.

Often, though, people eat quickly, not taking time to be aware of the tastes in their mouths. The following exercise will help you be more mindful of the different tastes when you eat as well as to slow down so you aren't gulping in food so quickly.

Time Needed: **10 MINUTES**
Location: **KITCHEN OR DINING ROOM**

Before you get started, choose three foods that have different tastes and different textures. Here are some ideas:

○ A cracker or piece of bread

○ A grape, strawberry, slice of apple, or banana

○ A piece of chocolate

○ A raisin

○ A carrot, red pepper, or piece of lettuce

Place the foods in front of you.

To begin, look at the food. Notice the color of each item. See how colorful different foods are. Observe which are smooth or rough.

Now, feel the food using your hands (make sure they are clean!). Do some foods feel mushy or hard? Are they smooth or ridged?

Pick up the food and smell it. Which ones smell sweet or sour?

Take one of the food items and put it in your mouth. Before you begin chewing the food, let your tongue taste the flavor. Chew slowly. Notice if the food melts in your mouth or if you have to chew it many times to soften it. Do you like it? Do you love it? Why or why not?

Now, take the second food and put it in your mouth. Again, chew slowly and experience the food. Does it taste different from the first? How so?

Take the third food and repeat the steps above.

After you've eaten all three pieces of food, reflect on how you experienced each one. Did you like one better than the other? Why or why not?

NOTICE YOUR INNER VOICE

What you say—both in your head and to others—shapes how you see the world.

Sometimes it's easy to put yourself down. Maybe you sometimes think, *I'm not good enough to play on the sports team* or *No one likes me because I'm not smart or pretty enough.* When you tell yourself negative things over and over, you start to act like or believe they are true. Also, when you criticize yourself or complain all the time to others, then people may become annoyed with you or view you in a negative way.

Sometime kids think it's cool to put down others, but remember that they do this because they don't feel so great about themselves.

Try being positive with your words, and see if your life and relationships change.

Here is a game you can do with a friend, sibling, or even your parents. The purpose is to become aware of your thoughts and what you say to others. You may also enjoy doing this by yourself.

Time Needed: **1 HOUR OR 1 DAY!**
Location: **ANYWHERE**

Decide that for one hour (or a full day), you are not going to criticize or complain about anything—not in your head or to someone else.

Whenever someone playing this game (including you) criticizes or complains, that person gets a point. (You have to be honest and admit to the other person about what's going on in your head. And if you are doing this with your parents, keep track of their words, too!)

See who has the least points at the end of the hour or day. And, more importantly, think about if you felt differently at the end of the time. Was it hard or easy not to complain or criticize anyone or yourself? Do you tend to criticize and complain without even thinking about it?

When you're more conscious of your inner dialogue, you will notice how what you say to yourself and others can change your mood. If you tell yourself, *I am tired*, then you will feel tired. If you tell yourself, *I am not smart*, then you won't feel that smart. But if you tell yourself *I am happy*, you will find reasons to be happy. If you tell yourself, *I love and have loved ones*, you will appreciate the meaningful relationships you have in your life.

NOTICE

Notice Your Words to Others

· · · · ·

What you say to others and how you act around them can make them feel happy or sad. Sometimes you may make a casual comment about someone's clothes or shoes—like "those shoes are really weird"—and not realize that it affects that person deeply. After hearing what you thought was an innocent comment or observation, that person may decide never to wear those shoes again.

When you give feedback to someone else, when you comment on a social media post, when you are talking to your friends or siblings, you should be mindful and take a moment before you speak to think about if you are being kind and helpful with what you are saying or if your words could be interpreted negatively.

It's important that you become more aware of your words and how they will affect others. The key thing to remember is: Before you speak, *think*:

T*: Is it* **true***?*

H*: Is it* **helpful***?*

I*: Is it* **inspiring***?*

N*: Is it* **necessary***?*

K*: Is it* **kind***?*

With practice, you will soon realize the power of your words! You will also notice that those around you will like being with you more, will consider you a good friend or sibling, and will likely seek your honest opinion about things in the future, knowing you'll be mindful of their feelings.

Just STOP for a Moment

· · · · ·

Do you ever find yourself in a stressful situation? Your heart starts racing and you start panicking. Maybe you slept late. You had planned to study for a history test during breakfast and now you don't have time! Or you are getting ready for your dance rehearsal and suddenly you can't remember your routine!

When you are feeling panicked, sometimes slowing down actually helps you get back in control of a situation. Imagine you are in a stressful situation. You just found out that your friend is having a sleepover and you were not invited. Your heart is starting to feel heavy with sadness and you may even feel as though you'll start to cry.

Here is a tip that can help you manage stressful situations and can be used whenever you start to feel panicked. Just remember: STOP!

S: *Just* **stop.**

T: *Then* **take three breaths.**

O: *Next,* **observe your body and your thoughts.**

P: *Finally, you can* **proceed.**

This exercise won't take the pain or the fear away, but what it will do is help your body and brain to feel stronger in order to deal with the situation. It will help get you in the zone to focus on what needs to be done.

And, in a real situation, it may stop you from saying something mean to your friend, hurting her just because you feel hurt. You may realize that just because she invited others over doesn't mean she's not your friend, too. You may discover, calmly, that your relationship with her was not what you thought it was and that you need to make some changes.

When you STOP before speaking or taking action, you won't be as likely to approach a situation with your fight-or-flight response; instead, you'll approach the situation thoughtfully and will be prepared to come up with better solutions, responses, and, ultimately, outcomes.

Test Jitters

· · · · ·

You have studied really hard for your upcoming test, but when you sit down to actually take it, the butterflies in your stomach are whizzing like crazy! Your hands are sweating and you may even be shaking a bit! You think, *Tests are the worst and I'm going to flunk this one!*

This is the time to breathe in and out a few times. Just know that you can only do your best and that's okay.

If you want to try to prevent those test-taking jitters, before jumping straight into your test, try to do the following to help your body and mind relax:

· Place a hand on the test.

· Take a deep breath in and count to three. One. Two. Three.

· Blow out that anxiety as you count to three again. One. Two. Three.

· Now, with your hand on the test, say to yourself: *I got this. I got this.*

· Proceed!

TRANSITIONS

Over the next few years, you will go through many transitions. Your body will change. You may leave elementary school and start middle school or high school. You may join a new sports team or dance or theater program. Your friends may seem different, or you may want to meet new people. Your family may also go through changes.

When you are experiencing changes, your whole world can feel wobbly and unstable. You may not know who to turn to for help because you might feel like the people in your life are changing, too.

Here is an exercise that may help you remember that even though things are changing and in flux, the inside part of you—your soul—is always there and constant.

Time Needed: **15 MINUTES**
Location: **ANYWHERE**

Sit comfortably. It may be helpful to close your eyes.

Take a deep breath. Breathe in. Pause. Breathe out.

In this meditation, you are going to focus on the PAUSE.

Put your attention on your heart, and as you breathe steady, feel that quiet, peaceful space when you pause: Breathe in. Pause, noting how peaceful it feels. Breathe out.

Now, think about what you were doing just before you sat down to meditate. See what you were doing, who you were talking to, what you were thinking about. As you play it out in your mind, take a moment and feel yourself doing that activity. See yourself breathing and note the PAUSE between breaths as you envision the activity.

Flash back to this morning when you were eating breakfast. Again, see the food, see who you were sitting with, and see what you were doing or talking about. Feel yourself breathing, and note the PAUSE between breaths.

Take a moment and recognize that you are the same right now as you were just before you sat down to meditate and that you were the same this morning when you were eating breakfast. You can feel the real you in that pause between breaths.

Think back to a week ago and remember something you were doing—perhaps it was playing a soccer game or taking a test at school. As you remember that moment, connect to the pause between your breaths. The same you was there last week, just as it is right now.

Remember an event from last year. Perhaps it was your birthday party. Connect again to the pause between your breaths as you replay that event. Feel the you inside that is experiencing that event.

Remember a time from when you were a baby. You can imagine what it was like being held by your mother or crawling and discovering the world for the first time. Connect to the pause between your breaths as you remember—know that in that pause, in that space between breaths, you were the same then as you are in this moment.

Now, stop thinking, and breathe in and out. In. Pause. Out. Remember the pause.

Make a decision, right now, that you will remember what it feels like in that moment as you move forward in life.

This is the real you—your soul; the part of you that stays with you forever.

No matter what changes on the outside, you can always find this part of you in the pause between your breaths. Let it be your anchor. Know that changes may be hard, but you can always remain stable in the midst of chaos.

BE AWARE OF LISTENING

When you are having a conversation with others, you speak and you listen. Or hopefully that's the case. Sometimes you may be speaking and you sense that the other person isn't listening to you. Remember that it's possible you do the same to others at times. Someone may be telling you something really important, but you are thinking about something else and not really listening. Or, maybe you try to be helpful by sharing your thoughts on something, but what you really should be doing is listening to what the other person is telling you.

When you fully listen to others, you hear more. You sense what they are telling you, even beyond their words. You learn more and feel more connected as well. And by your example, others may listen to you better, too.

Conscious listening takes practice. When you become aware of how you listen, it is amazing to notice your body language and how natural it is to interrupt others. You also begin to notice people's moods and motivations beyond their words—you become more socially aware!

Tell a parent, sibling, or caretaker that you want to try the following conscious listening exercise with him or her.

Time Needed: **5 MINUTES**
Location: **ANYWHERE**

First, set up a quiet environment for your conversation. Turn off the radio or television. If you have a phone or computer in front of you, put it on mute or stow it away. Ask the person you are doing the exercise with to also put their devices away.

Tell them that while they speak, you are just going to listen. Ask them to tell you about something that happened today. And as they tell you their story, don't interrupt them. Don't feel like you need to say anything—don't even say yes or no, and don't even nod. Just fully listen to them. Hear their story. Understand how they feel.

When they are done, switch roles.

Ask them to listen to your story, again without distractions. Ask them not to interrupt you and to just fully listen.

Once you both have shared your stories, now you can react and share your ideas about what each other has said—tell each other how you feel.

It is important for you to practice listening, mindfully, throughout the day. See if it changes how you interact with friends, teachers, and other people in your life when you stop and listen fully before responding.

A DIFFERENT PERSPECTIVE

Sometimes you may find yourself becoming frustrated when you believe strongly in something and a friend, teacher, or even a stranger or parent disagrees with you. You could be looking at or have access to the same information, and yet you have different feelings, opinions, or action plans for the information you are processing!

The following is a classic story that may help you better understand that people have different perspectives about similar issues and that's okay:

Five blind men lived in a village. These men were considered the wisest men in the community because they were able to understand people and situations by truly listening. They heard stories from the travelers who came through their village and would teach others life lessons.

However, they had been having one argument for years. They had heard about elephants—how they could trample through forests, carry huge trees, and make loud noises that scared people from far away. But they also knew that the king let his daughter travel on the elephant. So they argued about whether the elephant was a vicious creature or a gentle one. They argued and argued about this for many years until the villagers grew so frustrated that they organized a visit to the palace so they could meet the elephant once and for all.

The first blind man approached the animal, felt its leg with his hands, and said, "It is like a tree. Feel how it is rooted strongly to the ground. See, I was right. It is a strong and fierce animal."

The second blind man felt the elephant's tail and, stroking it, he said, "You are wrong! This is just like a piece of rope! It can do no harm."

The third blind man felt the elephant's trunk, jumped back, and said, "Beware! This is like a big, powerful snake! The king must be crazy to let the princess come near this creature!"

The fourth blind man felt the tusk, backed away, and said, "It is like a spear, sharp and powerful! I agree with my friend that it is too dangerous."

The fifth blind man felt the elephant's ear, smiled, and said, "Oh lovely! It is like a fan that must cool and soothe our princess. Absolutely beautiful!"

The wise men now got more and more frustrated, arguing louder and louder! They created such a commotion that the king was awakened from his nap and

approached them. As he listened to their explanations about the elephant, he chuckled and kindly told them, "You each touched only one part of the animal. If you put the parts together, I am sure you will be able to see the whole thing."

The wise men were silenced and each thought deeply about the king's words. On their journey home, they listened to each other, put the pieces together, and realized what a magnificent creature they had encountered.

Below is an exercise that may help you understand how people form different perspectives. It's a good reminder that everyone chooses the information that shapes how each of us sees the world.

Time Needed: **10 MINUTES**
Location: **ANYWHERE**

Get a piece of paper and a pen. On the paper, draw an elephant. Don't worry—you don't have to be an artist to do this.

In your imagination, approach the elephant and gently feel its trunk. How does it feel? Write down your answer to this and each subsequent question.

Now, slide your hand along its ivory tusk. How would you describe it?

Try to put your arms around one of its four legs. Can you do it? How big does it feel?

Pet its big, flappy ear. How would you describe what you are touching?

Feel its long, hairy tail. Does it remind you of anything?

Look at each description you've written down. Do any of them by themselves describe the elephant?

Learning to be comfortable with different perspectives may be one of the most important strengths you can build. As you grow older, you will realize that people react differently to the same situation and that people have different religious, political, and social views. Most people, based on their experiences, truly believe and are attached to their perspectives. You could be an important bridge in bringing people together and, like the king in this story, helping them understand why there are many points of view.

TRUSTING YOUR INNER VOICE

All of us feel peer pressure at times to do things to fit in with the crowd. It is natural. You want people to like you. You don't want to look foolish. You want others to think you are cool and you want to have friends.

But whenever you do something that doesn't feel right, you know inside that you don't feel good. Perhaps it is something you are ashamed to tell your parents about or that you feel guilty about. These feelings can then build up and create stress in your life.

In this next exercise, remind yourself that you are good enough, that you know the answers to the questions you have, and that you have the strength to do what's right and what you feel comfortable doing.

Time Needed: **2 MINUTES**
Location: **ANYWHERE THERE IS A MIRROR**

Stand in front of a mirror in your room or bathroom or hold a mirror in front of you in a private space.

Look at yourself in the mirror. Make eye contact with yourself.

Say the following phrases:

> *I am beneath no one, and no one is beneath me.*
>
> *I am independent of the good and bad opinion of other.*
>
> *I trust myself to make the right decisions for me.*

Look deep into your own eyes and know these phrases to be true.

Take a deep breath, in and out, and let those phrases sink in.

So the next time you find yourself in a situation where you feel pressured to do something that doesn't feel right, take a deep breath. Flash back to this moment in front of the mirror, and ask yourself, *What is the right decision for me?* Then, you'll be able to make the right choice for yourself and you'll feel good about it.

Bully Beware

· · · · ·

How you present yourself to the world gives a message about how you will allow yourself to be treated by others. Unfortunately, people who don't feel good about who they are will play out their insecurities by bullying others.

Being mindful of how you act and being aware of your surroundings can be an important step to avoiding those who act mean and hurtful—and can keep you from being a bully yourself! As you go through your day, remember the following things:

· Be aware of your body language.
Walk tall, with your head held up high. In your head,
you can repeat this phrase: I am beneath no one.

· Be mindful of where you are. Avoid being alone in places
where bullies may find and target you.

· Be mindful of how you react to others. Bullies get their power
when they see their victims get upset. When you are more aware of
what gets you upset, you can find ways to control how you
express your emotions outwardly. You can take the satisfaction away from
the bully if you don't react emotionally to their words or actions.

· Be aware of the power of your voice. If you are confronted by a bully
and cannot walk away in that moment, use your voice. Most bullies want you
to be scared of them. Instead of confronting them, perhaps try
asking them what they are upset about or why they need to show power
in this way. You may just confuse them enough to stop
their bullying and get out of the situation.

· Ask for help. You do not have to confront a bully alone.
You can tell a teacher or trusted adult to help you find
a solution to the problem and don't feel that you have
to keep silent if you are being bullied.

If you know deep down inside that sometimes you are the bully, ask yourself, *Why am I doing this?* Be honest. Does it make you feel more powerful? Do you feel guilty after? Guilt creates stress that will never make you feel good about yourself. Most importantly, does it make you feel happy and connected? Know that you can always change your behavior, and people will respect you for doing the right thing.

Intents

· · · · ·

An intent is what you want in your life.

You may want certain things, like a new Lego set or a bike. Or you may want to take a trip somewhere with your family or go to a concert or see your favorite sports team with your friends.

You may have a specific goal, like doing well on a test or winning a game.

But an intent is different from a goal that you can check off when done.

An intent is more like how you want to feel in your whole life. Some intents include being:

- happy
- loved
- inspired
- valued
- heard

Think about some of the feelings you want in your life. Write them down on a piece of paper or in a journal. Or, you can draw the colors and images that represent how you would like to feel.

Intents come from your deepest desires—that's why it is so important to think about what you *really* want in your life. If you think about wanting lots of friends, you are actually setting the intent to be connected with others.

When you set an intent, you put your focus and energy into making it happen. If you want to feel connected, you grow courage to talk to new people, to sit with a new group at lunch, or to invite someone over for a playdate. Intents lead to actions and creating the life you truly want to live!

How Does an Intent Work?

· · · · ·

Imagine planting a seed in a garden. You may know that you are planting a seed for a rosebush, but you don't know exactly what the roses will look like when they grow.

You dig a hole in the ground, preparing the soil for the seed. Once you put the seed in the dirt, you cover it up. You water the seed. You let the sun nurture it. You give it time to grow.

If you dig up the seed to look at it every day then it is not going to grow. You have to trust that nature will take care of it—that the work you do will help it grow and that one day you will see the first bud.

In your life, when you set an intent, you plant a seed.

You may not know exactly how that seed will grow or what it will look, smell, and feel like. But because you know that the intent is important to you, you will start to find ways to make it grow and flourish.

Setting an Intent

• • • • •

You can set an intent for how you want to feel each and every day.

Maybe one day you want to have more energy, another day you want more alone time, and another day you want to feel more connected to your friends or family. Setting an intent in the morning can help you feel anchored for the whole day.

Imagine a ship that is sailing on a rough ocean. The anchor helps the ship stay in place even as the wind and waves try to move it. Your intent is like that anchor. When you set it, consciously and confidently, then when things get difficult or uncertain, your intent will prevent you from giving up or floating away. That intent is deep down inside you, reminding you that you have the strength to keep going!

Setting an intent is super simple, just follow these steps:

1. Think about how you want to feel today.

2. Say to yourself, "My intent is _____."

3. Imagine the intent being planted inside of you, just like a seed, and let go, trusting that today it will blossom into something special for you.

If you are comfortable sharing your intent with others, you can ask for their support in reaching it for the day. You could tell your intent to your mom, dad, sibling, friend, caretaker, or teacher. You could ask them what their intent is today, too, and offer to help support them in reaching it. But if you are more comfortable keeping it private, that's okay, too.

You can write down your intent and keep the paper in your pocket so you can be reminded of it at any time. Or you can write it in a journal and see how your intent changes or stays the same from day to day. What can be really fun is to see how your intent played out—did something happen today that was random or magical or silly but actually supported your intent? You may be freaked out when you start to notice

how people and situations suddenly seem to remind you of your intent without you even trying to do anything.

Who Am I?

· ○ · · ·

Knowing who you are helps anchor you for everything you do in life.

Who you are inside stays the same year after year, as you grow up, meet new people, and transition to new places.

If you know who you are, and are confident about it, then you also are not as affected by the words and actions of other people.

Grab a sheet of paper and write down words to the following prompts:

○ Who am I?

○ List who you are in relation to other people
(for example, daughter, brother, friend, etc.).

○ List who you are by the activities you do
(for example, soccer player, pianist, dancer, etc.).

○ List who you are on the outside
(for example, Indian, Latino, girl with long black hair, tall, etc.).

○ List what you feel like on inside—what are the qualities that make you, you
(for example, positive, hopeful, talkative, shy, etc.).

○ List how you see yourself on this planet
(for example, as a part of nature, a child of God, spirit, etc.).

Now, think about what makes you, you!

You may be a soccer player this year, but if you decide not to play soccer anymore, will you still be you?

If you cut your long black hair much shorter, will you be different? Perhaps you will feel different, but inside will you still be you?

And, while you will always be a daughter or brother or friend, your role and how you interact with people may change. But inside, will you be the same?

Breathe deeply, and feel inside who you are. Feel how that quiet place where you connect with your breath will always be with you, no matter how your role or looks or the things you do change. When you can feel who you are in this way, when things get tough, when you start feeling insecure or left out, you can just breathe and feel stronger again.

What Do I Want?

Here is an easy but difficult question to ask yourself: What do you want?

If you could have anything in the world to make you happy, what would it be?

Knowing what will make you happy is the first step to getting it in your life. You may want material things, like a new video game or a certain pair of sneakers. You may want experiences, like a vacation to Hawaii or going to a baseball game with your parents and siblings. You may want to have lots of friends and close relationships with your siblings. You may strive to be a basketball player, professional dancer, or coder.

If you think deeply about what you want, you can break that down into the qualities that you want in your life, like happiness, connection, belonging, inspiration, and a sense of purpose.

Now, think about what makes you happy and ask yourself these questions:

° What are the material things that
will make me happy?

° What are the experiences that
will make me happy?

° Who are the people that make me happy?

° What goals will make me happy?

° What qualities will make my life
happy and fulfilled?

Over the course of your life, you may find that the material things and experiences and what you want to be when you grow up changes, but the *qualities* that you want in your life remain somewhat constant. So, if you decide you want to be happy, then you can figure out today what will make you happy. If you want adventure, you can ask your parents to take you somewhere new. Or, if you want connection, you can think about how you can reach out to someone today.

How Can I Serve?

• • • • •

Meditation, mindfulness, and breathing practices are things you do by yourself to give you peace and strength. Taking care of yourself is important for your health and happiness. Self-care is not selfish; rather, it is about being smart and healthy.

It is important to know and strive for the qualities you want in your life, but when you are feeling confident, fulfilled, and strong, you will naturally find that you want to reach out to others.

Ultimately, mindfulness and meditation practices are about serving both yourself and others. You will have an even fuller life if you are helping others. When you do something for someone else—make someone smile and feel loved—you will find that you are doing something meaningful and have a sense of purpose.

Everyone has his or her own way of serving others. If you can serve happily, using your strengths, you'll likely feel that your life has purpose and that can feel magnificent!

Find a piece of paper or grab your journal and write the following, filling in the blanks:

How can I serve . . .

Myself:

My Family:

My Friends:

My Teachers:

My Community:

You may not be able to do all these things yourself. In fact, if you ask others for help or you serve with them, you may find that it's even more fun and meaningful.

After you've tried serving one of the above groups, add in your thoughts and reflections to your paper or journal and keep this in mind as you continue to find ways to serve each day.

WHAT AM I GRATEFUL FOR?

Gratitude means being thankful for what you have in your life. When you think about what you are grateful for, you will literally change your brain to think about things more positively in your life. You'll see things differently and make choices to be happier and feel more connected.

When you are grateful, your body releases chemicals that make you happier and calmer. Even in your darkest, saddest, most depressed moments, you can probably find something to be grateful for. And you don't have to be grateful for material things. In fact, you can be grateful for your breath, for the earth that nurtures you, or for people in your life who love you.

Right now, think of one thing that you are grateful for. Put your attention on your heart, and say to yourself, "I am grateful for _____."

Here is an exercise to try for the next week to help you become more grateful and to recognize what is really important to you:

Time Needed: **5 MINUTES**
Location: **IN YOUR BED**

Every night before you go to sleep, think about three things that you are grateful for. If you want, you can write them down in a journal. Or you can share them with your parents or a sibling.

Choose three specific things every day for one week. Perhaps they are the same; perhaps they change every day. It doesn't matter. Just make the decision to state what you are grateful for every day and spend a little time reflecting on those three things.

Try this exercise for one week and see if you feel different. You may also find that you want to express or share your gratitude with others—maybe thank your teacher for a great class or leave a note by your mom's coffee mug to thank her for making you lunch.

For a second week, see if you can find new things to be grateful for. You will start to discover new things in your life that make you feel happy and connected, guaranteed.

WHO ARE MY HEROES?

Everyone has certain people in their life that they admire and who they may even think of as heroes. They may be people who are part of your everyday life, like your grandmother. Or they may be someone in your neighborhood, like a policeman.

They may even be a fictional character who is inspiring, like Spider-Man or a character from a Harry Potter book. Or perhaps it is someone from history who changed the world—like Martin Luther King Jr. or Mother Teresa. They may be a person from your religion like the Imam at your mosque, your priest, or your rabbi. Perhaps it is a more publicly spiritual person, like the Dalai Lama or the Pope. Or maybe your hero is your god or goddess who you pray to every day.

When you honor your heroes, you recognize that you want to be like them. You want to have the good, strong qualities that make them who they are and that can inspire who you can become.

Use the following meditation to think about your heroes:

Time Needed: **5 MINUTES**
Location: **ANYWHERE**

Have a piece of paper and pen by your side.

Sit comfortably and take a deep breath. In and out.

Think of the people—either real or fictional—who you identify as your heroes.

Write down their names.

Now, think about the qualities that person brings to the world that you admire. Next to their name, write down what they do or what qualities they have that you admire.

Finally, think of one thing you can do in the next week that reflects the quality you admire in you hero.

Write it down, and once you've completed it, write down what you did so you can see that you, too, can be just like those you admire.

Your Special Place

• • • • •

Creating a special place that is just your own can be a powerful exercise. Once you have started collecting meaningful things and putting them in your special spot, you will find that you can visit that place and feel secure, loved, and reminded of what makes you happy.

   To create a special place, just do the following:

1. Choose a place in your house that you can make your own. It may be in the corner of your room or even a drawer or shelf somewhere in your house. It should be a place where you can tell others that this space belongs to and is special for you.

2. Collect a few physical objects that are important to you for your space. Objects may include:

• Photographs

• Your special stuffed animal from when you were a baby

• A gift someone gave you

- A souvenir from a trip

- A poem

- A birthday card from a relative
or your best friend

- A religious symbol that is important to you

3. You may find that you have lots of things or too few. In the beginning, the fewer things you choose, the better. You may want to decorate the space with drawings or fabric that makes you feel peaceful and secure.

4. Once you have finished, sit in front of your objects and take a deep breath. Feel the love and connection and happiness that these objects bring to or hold in your life. As you breathe in, remember that they represent those qualities. (Even if you didn't have the objects in front of you, you can still feel the same.)

Try to look at your special place once a day or at least once a week. Every time you visit it and look at the objects, take a deep breath, breathing in the love, connection, and happiness you feel every time you visit that one place that's all your own.

Over time, you can keep adding things (or taking them away) from your special place as you grow and change as an individual.

Color! Color!

· · · · ·

Do you remember when you were really young and you could sit and get lost in a coloring book for hours? You could choose which colors you'd use to fill in particular shapes, making a picture your own with the splash of colors that you chose.

Coloring isn't just for little kids anymore. And, in fact, it may help you relax, work out problems, and feel creative. Coloring allows you to focus and be flexible at the same time. You can draw inside or outside the lines! You can also choose colors that will give your picture your own unique twist.

Here are a few inspirations for coloring activities:

- A mandala is a geometric pattern, often in a circle, that can let your mind wander while coloring. You may notice mandalas in many paintings from ancient traditions. Try drawing your own mandala—be creative with patterns and colors!

• Nature has healing powers—fresh air, the sun, water, and the earth are grounding. Think of a place in nature where you feel free and happy. Draw this place that brings you peace. Keep your drawing as a reminder of how good you can feel.

• Find old coloring books you may have lying around your house. You may find empty pages inside, so take an afternoon and just color, remembering how creative you felt when you were a little kid with a box of crayons.

You Can Create the Life You Want

• • • • •

At times, you may feel alone, helpless, and confused about your relationships with friends and family. You may feel that you are struggling at school and just don't enjoy your days.

Life can be hard. People you love can hurt you. You might feel alone. But just remember, everyone struggles through life at one time or another. If you can remember that, you can then create the life you want by the way that you react to situations, and you will then get through tough times with more ease. Here is an example: A classmate at school has been teasing you. It is normal to feel hurt and maybe scared because you feel like you are being bullied. Perhaps you are nervous about what others may think of you. But you could feel that way and also make a decision to do something about it.

You have the choice to tell your parents, a teacher, or trusted adult what is going on. Or you can choose to confide in a friend and, together, decide that you will ask this bully why they are pushing you around. Or you can decide to let it be, knowing that the situation may continue but that you will try not to let it bother you.

Having done the exercises in this book, you are transitioning from making decisions out of fear (remember that fight-or-flight reaction?) to thoughtfully choosing to do things that are healthier and safer for you. When you are faced with a difficult situation, remember to breathe deeply, think about different perspectives and ways of doing things, and come up with a solution that feels safe, calm, and right for you.

THE POWER OF YOUR MIND

Your mind is a fascinating part of you. It shapes how you see the world, how you learn, how you react to situations, and how you interact with others. You can change the way your mind works through good habits and practices. You can even create new experiences just by thinking and imagining them!

The following is a very simple exercise to help you realize how just thinking about something creates a reaction or experience in your body:

Time Needed: **2 MINUTES**
Location: **ANYWHERE**

Close your eyes. Perhaps you see images or color as you settle into having your eyes closed.

Decide in your head that you want it to be dark. Think blue. Can you imagine blue in your mind?

Now, think pink.

Have the colors inside, even with your eyes closed, changed?

*Notice how **you**, the one who is imagining the colors, can control what's happening inside.*

Imagine a rose. Can you see it? Can you imagine the smell?

Imagine a lemon. Can you see the yellow in your head? Can you imagine what it tastes like if you squeeze the lemon juice on your tongue?

Imagine a tree that you see every day. How does it look in the different seasons?

If you can create images in your head, you can also choose your thoughts, actions, and emotions! And that's a very helpful way to approach each day and each interaction you have with your family, friends, and even strangers.

How Do You View the Glass?

• ○ • ○ •

You have the power to choose how you look at the world—whether you are positive or negative about the things happening around you and about your place among those things.

Look at this glass.

Describe what you see. Do you see the glass as half full? Or, do you see it as half empty?

Many people use this example as a way they see the world. When you are in an uncomfortable situation, do you approach it as a negative thing (a pessimist), or do you see an opportunity to change something, making it more positive (an optimist)?

A pessimist is someone who usually sees the glass as half empty. When there is a problem, a pessimist can only complain and think about how the world is coming to an end. Imagine you have planned your birthday party picnic at your favorite park. You have organized the games, the treats, and time for everyone to run around and have fun. The day comes, but it's raining! A pessimist would be upset and angry, cancel the party, and think that no one will ever be her friend again.

An optimist, however, is someone who usually sees the glass as half full. If you are an optimist, you may also get upset at first about the rainy birthday. But then you would think of other things you could do. Maybe you could have friends come to your home instead. Some games could still be played, and the treats will still work. The optimist may even see it as an opportunity for friends to have fun talking, learn more about each other, and grow closer in a more relaxed atmosphere.

Look at the glass again.

There is another way to look at this glass. This time, look at it as totally full. After all, it is half full of water and half full of air. Imagine if you always saw your world as full. There will be highs and lows, but you can learn and grow from every experience. Yes, sometimes you are super happy and other times you are sad and lonely. But life works like that—the difficult times make you stronger and make the good times even better. It's a big idea, but one that just may be worth thinking about!

Choosing How You
Treat Others

• • • • •

Sometimes, everyone can be mean to someone else. Maybe you are mean on purpose. Maybe you hurt someone's feelings by mistake or didn't even realize that you upset someone. But you know that because of what you did, someone is sad and unhappy.

Usually when we are mean, we know, inside of us, that we did something wrong.

There are a few ways you can act when you have been mean, on purpose or accidentally:

• You can pretend you didn't do anything wrong
(even though inside you know you did).

• You can find a reason to blame the other person.

• You can feel guilty but keep quiet,
hoping the other person will forget what you did.

• You can make a choice to take
responsibility and apologize.

You have the ability to create the sort of relationships you want in your life. And that includes when you have not been the best child or friend or student that you know you can be.

So if you hurt someone, you can choose to take responsibility and say, "I'm sorry." You can reach out to someone you know who is hurting. You can do something special for someone, even if they don't know you did it.

When you take responsibility for your own actions, you feel in control of the life you want. You don't waste time feeling guilty or regretting that you didn't do something. You know inside that you can make things better. Even if the other person doesn't accept your apology, you will know that you tried and chose to try to make amends. And then you can move forward without guilt, and with the intention of being nicer in the future.

IMAGINE WHO YOU CAN BE

- - - - - - - - - - -

When you were younger, did you ever dream that you could do anything you wanted to? Like be an astronaut who flies into the farthest galaxies and walks on planet surfaces.

Or a baseball player who hits the winning home run in the World Series.

Or the editor of a successful fashion magazine.

Or a doctor who saves the lives of children all over the world.

Or a princess of a magical, delicious land made of candy.

Or a wizard who lords over a universe full of dragons, knights, and castles.

When you dream about things, your imagination creates colors, sensations, and emotions. You feel excited, more confident, and ready to take on the world!

But, sadly, as you grow older, sometimes you let go of those dreams. They may seem too hard or require too much work to attain. Sometimes other people will tell you that the dream is silly or that you will never be able to actually do it.

You might lose that confidence that you once had—the bright-eyed outlook that made you feel like you could do anything as a little kid. As people grow older, they sometimes lose that sense of magic that they once believed in so easily.

In this exercise, let your imagination take over like it used to do when you were a little kid. Be as magical, fun, and silly as you want to be.

Time Needed: **10 MINUTES**
Location: **ANYWHERE YOU FEEL COMFORTABLE**

Do this exercise in a place where you feel comfortable and can even move or dance or act out without feeling self-conscious. You may feel more comfortable doing it with no one else around, with your eyes closed, or by simply writing it down on paper. Whatever feels most natural to you, do that.

Think about something you would like to do or be in the future. It could be a profession or a fairy-tale character that you know of or just made up.

First, imagine that you are looking at yourself, like you are watching your-self acting in a movie.

Imagine what you look like. Are you older or the same age? What are you wearing? What is your hairstyle like? What do you feel like physically?

Now, create a place—the setting for this act. Where are you? Inside or outside? Is it a familiar place or somewhere you have never been before? Don't leave out any details!

What time is this taking place? Is it in the future? Perhaps in ancient times?

What is the temperature like outside? Is it sunny or dark?

Remember: you can create any place or setting that you want.

Now, decide what you are doing in this setting. The beauty of this exercise is that you can do anything you want to here.

Imagine a scene, like in a movie, of you doing whatever you want to do in this place. This is your creation.

As you create the scene, watch yourself. What do you decide to do once you are here? Feel proud of what you are doing, of who you are in this scene.

Take a few minutes and really enjoy yourself.

As you continue your scene, make a slight shift. Now, focus on what you are feeling inside.

If you are doing what you really want, hopefully you are feeling happy, confident, and perhaps peaceful or super excited. Whatever you are feeling is just right for you.

Take a deep breath and let that feeling go through every part of your body. Let that feeling wander into your heart. Feel it in your hands, in your feet, in your face, and at the top of your head.

Take another breath as you get ready to leave this place. Take as much time as you would like, knowing that this place, this feeling, is always inside you. As you grow older, perhaps you will choose different dreams, but the you that is confident in this dream is always there inside of you, no matter what.

You have these feelings and capabilities inside you—you know it! Imagination is magical because you can create whatever you want to in your head. You can fly to the stars, singing at the top of your lungs and bringing along whoever you want. And with your imagination, you can feel strong, capable, and powerful.

You deserve all the peace, love, and joy in your life. Be bold in what you want, be comfortable in the quiet, creative moments, laugh and play, and create magic for yourself and others.

And don't forget: just breathe through it all!

AUTHOR'S NOTE

Meditation and mindfulness techniques can be found around the world and date back thousands of years. All the exercises in this book are commonly used, and it is difficult to specifically credit particular individuals.

I would like to recognize several teachers who have inspired me through their practices, books, and words.

My parents, Deepak and Rita Chopra, first learned Transcendental Meditation from Maharishi Mahesh Yogi, and our family practiced this technique for many years. My father, Dr. David Simon, and Roger Gabrielle later developed Primordial Sound Meditation, which is now taught at the Chopra Center for Wellbeing. The free 21-Day Meditation challenges offered through the Chopra Center and Oprah Winfrey are a great way to be led in meditations techniques on a regular basis. Learn more at www.chopra.com.

My parents taught my brother and me most of the mindfulness techniques in this book, and now my children and their friends are exposed to them at school and in their activities. Stories like the one of the wise men with the elephant have been told in many different ways over the centuries. Many of these techniques—like the Loving Kindness Meditation, mindful eating, and mindful walking—originated in Buddhist traditions. Jon Kabat-Zinn, Dr. Daniel J. Siegel, Susan Kaiser Greenland, Thich Nhatt Hanh, and Joan Halifax are some of the writers who have influenced my ongoing awareness of breathing and thoughts. Acronyms like STOP and THINK are now used in classrooms and organizations to help people mindfully approach stressful situations and communication. I feel fortunate to have learned from Dr. Lisa Miller, Linda Lantieri, and other professors at the Spirituality Mind Body Institute at Teachers College, Columbia University. They are great examples of the amazing teachers who work tirelessly and quietly every day to cultivate the inner lives of children, teachers, and parents.

As kids, my brother and I were guided by my father to think about intents—the qualities that we wanted to experience in our life. I invite kids, along with their parents, to visit www.intent.com to get inspiration and share your intents with others.

RESOURCES

The following are some of the books that my girls and I enjoyed reading together about health, meditation, and mindfulness:

The Care and Keeping of You #2: The Body Book for Older Girls, by Dr. Cara Natterson

Guy Stuff: The Body Book for Boys, by Dr. Cara Natterson

A Handful of Quiet: Happiness in Four Pebbles, by Thich Nhatt Hanh

I AM: Why Two Little Words Mean So Much, by Dr. Wayne Dyer

On My Way to a Happy Life, by Deepak Chopra with Kristina Tracy

Sitting Like a Frog: Mindfulness Exercises for Kids, by Elaine Snell and foreword by Jon Kabat-Zinn

What Does It Mean to Be Present?, by Rana DiOrio

Zen Shorts and *The Three Questions*, by John J. Muth

And, as a parent, these books are so helpful for me as my family continues to seek balance and happiness every day:

The Mindful Child and *Mindful Games*, by Susan Kaiser Greenland

Parenting from the Inside Out and *Brainstorm: The Power and Purpose of the Teenage Brain*, by Dr. Daniel J. Siegel

The Seven Spiritual Laws for Parents: Guiding Your Children to Success and Fulfillment, by Deepak Chopra

The Spiritual Child: The New Science of Parenting for Health and Lifelong Thriving, by Dr. Lisa Miller

ACKNOWLEDGMENTS

Before I started this book, I sat with my daughters, Tara (15) and Leela (12), and my nephew, Krishan (9), to get their ideas on the topics that would be interesting to them. So they really shaped everything you read here!

I'd like to thank the team at Running Press who had the idea for this book, and to my agent, Linda Loewenthal, who made it happen. I am dependent and grateful to MeLissa Gaverette, who impeccably manages my days, and to Geeta Singh, who launched my speaking career. Thank you to Carolyn and Felicia, and the team at the Chopra Center, who are always looking out for me. To Kanika and Candice, my anchors when it comes to advice and support on kids, but also life—thank you. And to all my mom friends—you are my village.

I would like to express my deepest gratitude to my parents, who gave me many gifts, including meditation.

And my unbounded love to my husband, Sumant Mandal, and our daughters, Tara and Leela, who fill every day with inspiration, joy, and purpose.